Performers

Irvine Welsh
&
Dean Cavanagh

This play is dedicated to the spirit and memories of Bradley Welsh (1971 – 2019) boxer, humanitarian, one of the chaps and a real performer.

And

Sebastian Horsley (1962 – 2010) artist, dandy, bohemian and a real performer.

Acknowledgements

Michael Hamlyn, Burning Wheel Productions, Sandy Lieberson, Jay Glennie, Craig Lawson, Matteo Sedazzari, Nick Moran, Eddie & Charlie Richardson, Mick Jagger and James Fox, Perry Benson, George Russo, Maya Gerber and Lewis Kirk.

Foreword

"It's true we did trip over gold. We, Donald and I, were prepared when we set out to make Performance; we were prepared to trip over gold and it is fair to say we did discover plenty on the film."

—Nic Roeg

Nic Roeg and Donald Cammell's Performance has been fertile mining ground for artists since its release in 1970. The films shapeshifting influence, blending gangsters and rock 'n' roll can be seen in the work of directors such as Lindsey Anderson, Jonathan Glazer, Stanley Kubrick, Martin Scorsese and Quentin Tarantino. Musicians including William Orbit, The Happy Mondays and Big Audio Dynamite have all used the score and film as reference points and samples in their songs. Jarvis Cocker, Don Letts, Bill Nighy, Paul Schrader and Stephen Woolley all told me of the profound effect the film had on their subsequent work and careers.

Also wishing to dig deep into the secrets of Performance were two "comical geezers" going by the names of Cavanagh and Welsh with their play Performers.

Kicking around ideas to collaborate on the two writers hit upon the idea of two gangsters – Welsh labelled them as "a couple of Chaps" – auditioning for the film Performance. "Dean and I got on a 60s kick and started talking about quintessential British movies that we'd loved from that decade, and Performance was a firm favorite of ours. I had seen it at the film society at Essex University. I went along initially because Jagger was in it, but it was so much more. It was fucking brilliant. I literally had never seen anything like it."

—Irvine Welsh

"The film, and equally the legend around the making of the film had a huge influence on me. Performance is a film that just keeps on giving; it offers up more secrets every time you watch it and along with Sexy Beast and 42 Inch Chest – both written by the brilliant Louis Mellis and David Scinto – it's the most accurate portrayal of London gangsters ever made. It's got that Pinteresque quality of razor sharp dialogue framed in colloquial verbal gymnastics and comic absurdity. There's a definite influence from Harold Pinter's The Homecoming and Dumb Waiters."

—Dean Cavanagh

The legend of Performance – the defining film of its era Performance – is either 'The most completely worthless film I have seen since I began reviewing' (Richard Schickel, Time Magazine 1970) or as championed in 2011 by Mark Cousins in his fifteen part TV series The Story of Film: An Odyssey '…not only the greatest seventies film about identity, if any movie in the whole Story of Film should be compulsory viewing for film makers, maybe this is it.'

These appraisals, over 40 years apart, showcase the critical about turn Performance has undertaken. Almost universally vilified upon its initial release – one notable exception was critic Derek Malcolm who championed the film, proclaiming it to be 'richly original, resourceful and imaginative, a real live movie' – Performance is now seen as one of the seminal films of the last 50 years.

Film historian and author Colin McCabe hails Performance as the best British film ever made. But even before its release the film studio funding it were repulsed by its violence, drug taking and sexual morality.

Performance is the film that arguably defines the late 60s in bohemian London. The blurred lines of reality and fiction came together to tell the story of Chas Devlin, a gangster and diligent enforcer of the will of his boss, Harry Flowers. Killing a rival puts the fragile status quo of the London underworld at risk and forces Chas to run and look for refuge until he can slip out of England. A Notting Hill townhouse owned by Turner, a burnt-out rock star would appear to be the ideal short-term hideaway. That is until Chas allows Turner's ménage à trois to mess with his identity even further.

American studio Warner Bros, wishing to tap into the burgeoning youth market, financed the production in their misguided belief that they were buying into a film depicting the optimism and energy of swinging London; a new A Hard's Day's Night (1964), complete with an accompanying album from the film's star, the biggest rock star on the planet, Mick Jagger.

Instead what they were handed was a heady cocktail of hallucinogenic mushrooms, sex – homosexual and three-way – violence, amalgamated identities and artistic references to Jorge Luis Borges, Magritte and Francis Bacon. Their star, Mick Jagger, failed to appear until nearly an hour into the film and only sung one song on the subsequent ground-breaking soundtrack by Jack Nitzsche.

After a string of number one singles – "(I Can't Get No) Satisfaction", "Get Off My Cloud", "Paint It Black", "Jumpin Jack Flash" – the Stones had released their seventh long player, Beggars Banquet, which longtime Stones engineer, Glyn Johns, called their "coming of age record", to universal acclaim but not a little controversy, with the backdrop of the civil unrest providing the impetus for "Sympathy for the Devil" and "Street Fighting Man".

Their success saw religious groups and the media label the Stones a corruptive influence on the God fearing youth, the accusation being that they were in league with the devil. This furore did little to dent their success, indeed the group's popularity only soared to even greater heights. And yet it was not sustaining their front man, Mick Jagger. The singer was looking to break into movies, as Jagger himself said, "to take on a role because it's more than just a pop star role."

Agent and soon to be film producer, Sandy Lieberson was enthusiastic about this move. "It was always going to be Mick as Turner, as an agent I knew Mick professionally, as well as being part of a group of friends that included Robert Fraser, Marianne, Keith and Anita, Kenneth Anger, Spanish Tony etc ... I had no doubts that Mick could do it. Donald, Nic and I were convinced he was completely right to play the rock star Turner in Performance. I knew that all the fame and notoriety surrounding him at that time of his life would be perfect."

What was imperative to Lieberson was that any film that he pursue with Cammell and Roeg, "would be influenced by the times we were living in. Into that mix went the political, social and psychological mood sweeping across the world and in particular for us in London."

The rising resentment against the ruling elite, thrown up and scattered across the globe in 1968, resulted in a seismic social and political change. "Performance was born out of that fervor and an understanding that we did not want to make a Hollywood movie. Donald, Nic and I wanted something that was going to rival the new wave cinema of France and Italy," says Lieberson.

It is no exaggeration to claim that 1968, the year the cameras rolled on Performance, was the year that changed the world forever. Christmas Eve saw the Apollo 8 spacecraft manned by Jim Lovell, Bill Anders and Frank Borman become the first manned spacecraft to orbit the moon. However, this proved to be a rare moment of good cheer in an otherwise challenging year.

Europe was rioting. Across France some ten million workers went on strike, virtually paralysing the country, in solidarity with students who had taken to the streets of Paris against the de Gaulle government, demanding reforms to their education system. "I happened to be in the Stones' office when Daniel Cohn-Bendit, leader of the '68 Paris riots and the student protest movement called after hearing "Street Fighting Man" to ask for Mick's support. I spoke to him and assured him that the Stones supported their cause," recalls Lieberson.

Central and Eastern Europe saw widespread protests against the restrictions on freedom of speech, resulting in the Prague Spring. The UK played host to frequent CND marches against the increasing fear of a nuclear holocaust. Conservative politician Enoch Powell's infamous anti-immigration 'river of blood' speech stoked further fires. The fear of an unwanted pregnancy had overshadowed any intimate relationship, but with the advent of the pill and the relaxation in 1967 of the draconian principle of only prescribing it to married women saw the UK finally attempt to shake off its Victorian attitudes to sex. The same year saw homosexuality decriminalized in England and Wales, despite the Home Secretary of the time, Roy Jenkins appearing to capture his government's attitude when he was quoted as saying during a parliamentary debate, "those who suffer from this disability carry a great weight of shame all their lives."

The Black Panther Party came to a wider public consciousness when two black American athletes, Tommie Smith and John Carlos, were sent home from the Mexico Olympic Games after raising their black gloved fists in the Black Power Salute during their medal ceremony. The year also saw the tragic assassinations of both Dr. Martin Luther King Jr. and Presidential hopeful, Senator Robert Kennedy, only adding further fuel to the civil rights protests raging across America. More American soldiers arrived home on US soil in body bags after the bloody Vietnam Tet Offensive, resulting in frequent demonstrations against further US involvement in the war.

"We also protested the Vietnam War here in London," remembered Lieberson. "Mick, Donald, Robert Fraser and I spent the afternoon cheering on Vanessa Redgrave in Grosvenor Square."

The '60s saw class barriers come crashing down as gangsters, pop performers and film stars mixed with aristocracy. London's Kings Road was full of androgynous looking males, eager to express their femininity. Co-directors, Cammell and Roeg brought all this together in a melting pot, which would go on to shake the film world. Their revolutionary language of imagery, brought to life with non-linear storytelling and Roeg's majestically lit cinematography, asked audiences to assemble a celluloid jigsaw puzzle in order to fully comprehend and unlock the film's mysteries.

In 1968 television audiences in the US witnessed the first interracial kiss when Star Trek's Captain Kirk kissed Lt. Uhura. The year before at the 1967 Academy Awards Bonnie and Clyde, In The Heat of the Night and The Graduate were all nominated for the Best Picture Oscar and the following year studios released genre defining films such as Rosemary's Baby, 2001: A Space Odyssey, Planet of the Apes, Teorema and The Boston Strangler.

So the times were a changing and it appeared that audiences were ready for a film with a great musical score, depicting the coming together of gangsters, rock 'n' roll, drugs and free love. However, these changes had gathered apace a little faster than Warner Bros. felt comfortable with. Viewing the film the hierarchy were horrified with their investment. Decrying the films graphic and decadent drug use, violence and sexual content – Jagger and co-star James Fox were seen on screen enjoying drug-fuelled sex with Anita and Michèle Breton – they refused to release the film. "They thought it was dirty," said producer Sandy Lieberson five decades later. Nic Roeg laughingly recalled fearing Warner Bros. were going to sue him.

"They found it pretty hard to understand – too much sex, too much violence. It was never going to appeal to a mass audience. But hey, it was never going too. I mean what were they expecting? Who read the script?" responded Jagger.

Two years of financial wrangling, threats from both the Studio, and 'Vice. And Versa' from Donald Cammell and Mick Jagger, ensued before the eventual release of Performance.

Set decorator Peter Young described the location shoot as a division of two distinct camps – the "straights", consisting of the older experienced film personnel and technicians, and the opposing camp made up of those who wished to partake in drugs: "a looser kinda lifestyle. The cool set". This highly charged atmosphere ensnared victims into its corruptive vortex. Despite telling me that Performance was the best performance he ever gave James Fox would leave the industry for ten years.

"When I had my Christian conversion in '69," he recalled, "My friend Johnny Shannon – Mob boss Harry Flowers in the film – asked me, 'Do you want me to sort them out, Jim?' I thought that it was so super of him. He thought I had got involved with a real heavy cult, one who were going to take my money and screw my mind."

The extraordinarily bright, handsome, louche and charming Donald Cammell would see his co-director Nic Roeg become lauded as one of the great filmmakers, whereas his own career floundered in Hollywood. And it was in the Hollywood Hills in relative obscurity aged 62 that he would place a revolver to his head and pull the trigger, after completing only three more films – Demon Seed (1977), White of the Eye (1987), Wild Side (1995).

Anita Pallenberg, the ultimate rock chick would begin her descent into drug addiction during filming, naively believing that she "had kept it from everyone."

And as for the star, what became of him? Mick Jagger survived the shoot in one piece, is still touring with The Rolling Stones and is still arguably the greatest rock 'n' roll singer on the planet.

The Stones' former manager, Andrew Loog Oldham stated "The Stones were not to the celluloid manor born". And yet Mick Jagger's cinematic debut as the reclusive rock star Turner is venerated as one of the greatest performances from a musician in film.

Sandy Lieberson once told me that a Nic Roeg film is only appreciated by a wider audience many years later and that chimes with Roeg's collaboration with Cammell. In keeping with a mature red wine it took a little patience and time for Performance to aerate before a wider audience caught on. Performance lives on and continues giving performances fifty years after its inception.

—Jay Glennie 2021

Jay Glennie is the author of Performance – the making of a classic featuring exclusive interviews with Mick Jagger, James Fox, Nic Roeg, Sandy Lieberson.

One Shot: the making of The Deer Hunter with contributions from Robert De Niro, Meryl Streep and Chris Walken

The making of Raging Bull with interviews with Robert De Niro, Martin Scorsese and Joe Pesci

Coming soon: The making of Trainspotting

Available via www.coattail-publications.com

Thy Will Shake Spears

As Sir Edward De Vere anonymously wrote under the pen name Shake-Speare – or he would have if he was perchance a Cockney rather than a Lord:

All the world's a stage,
and all the men and bints merely players;
They 'ave their exits and their entrances;
and one geezer in 'is time plays many parts,
his acts bein' seven ages. At first the bloody infant,
mewlin' and pukin' in the bleedin' nurse's arms;
and then the bloody winin' school-boy, wiv 'is sotchel
and shinin' mornin' boat race, creepin' like snail
unwillingly ter school. And then the bleedin' luvr,
sighin' like furnace, wiv a woeful ballad
made ter his mistress' eyebrow. Then a soldier,
full of strange oaffs, and bearded like the pard,
jealous in 'onour, sudden and quick in quarrel,
seekin' the bubble reputation.
Wiv mince pies severe and beard of formal cut,
full of wise sors and modern instances;
and so 'e plays 'is part. The bloomin' sixff age shifts
into the bloomin' lean and slipper'd pantaloon,
wiv spectacles on nose and pouch on side;
His yerffful 'ose, well sav'd, a world too wide.
For 'is shrunk shank; and 'is big manly voice,

turnin' again toward childish treble, pipes
and wistles in 'is sound. Last scene of all,
that ends this strange eventful 'istory,
is second childishness and mere oblivion;
sans teeff, sans mince pies, sans taste, sans evryfink.

PERFORMERS

Performers premiered on the 3rd of August 2017 at The Assembly Rooms as part of the Edinburgh International Fringe Festival.

WRITTEN BY
Dean Cavanagh & Irvine Welsh

DIRECTED BY
Nick Moran

PRODUCED BY
Michael Hamlyn & Burning Wheel Productions

CAST

Bert: George Russo
Alf: Perry Benson
Florence: Maya Gerber
Crispin: Lewis Kirk

SETTING: SMALL OFFICE IN OLD
COMPTON STREET, SOHO, 1968

CAST:

ALF – early 50's. East Londoner, working class, jovial.

BERT – early 30's. South Londoner, working class, moody, edgy.

FLORENCE – 16, pretty, petite, polite East Londoner, working class.

CRISPIN – mid 20's, public school educated, Bohemian.

VOICE: In the swinging and hallucinogenic London of 1968, visionary Scottish filmmaker Donald Cammell joined forces with cinematographer Nicolas Roeg to make "Performance". The film would star James Fox, Mick Jagger and Anita Pallenberg, but the casting process was frustrating for Cammell because he insisted on bringing "real villains" into the roles. This is the story of one of those auditions.

LIGHTS UP

A SMALL DUSTY OFFICE FULL OF PERIOD PHOTOGRAPHIC AND FILM EQUIPMENT: LIGHTS, CAMERAS, A FEW PROPS, A COUPLE OF REGULAR HOME SIZED PROJECTOR SCREENS, LIGHT METERS ETC... ALF – PORTLY, SUITED & BOOTED IN A BLACK TAILORED SUIT THAT IS A SIZE TOO SMALL, TOPPED OFF WITH A SILK DEEP RED POCKET SQUARE, IMMACULATE WHITE SHIRT, BRACES, BLACK SKINNY TIE, GOLD CUFFLINKS, PATENT LEATHER SHOES, THICK SQUARE FRAMED GLASSES. BERT – TALL, WELL BUILT, WEARING A CREAM CASHMERE TURTLE NECK UNDER A BLACK TAILORED SUIT, WITH MATCHING WAISTCOAT, BLACK PATENT LEATHER SHOES – ENTER THE ROOM WITH FLORENCE – WEARING A PAISLEY MINI SKIRT AND TWIN SET, KNEE HIGH WHITE LEATHER BOOTS, THICK EYE MAKE UP, HER HAIR IN A BOB STYLE. SHE'S CLEARLY EDGY WITH BERT.

FLORENCE

He won't be long Uncle. He said to show you in. I'll put the kettle on.

ALF

(to FLORENCE)

Thanks, petal. How you liking it here? They treating you good?

FLORENCE

Yeah, it's interesting. I like it.

ALF

"Interesting" eh? You hear that Bert? She's got an *interesting* job.

FLORENCE

My typing's not fast but I'm getting quicker. I might go to nightschool of an evening.

ALF

College, eh? You hear that, Bert? University!

FLORENCE

It's only nightschool, Uncle.

ALF

It's all the same thing. *Education*. You can't beat a good education, your Old Mum and Dad'll be really proud of ya.

FLORENCE

I better ... I think I heard the telephone.

ALF

The telephone eh? They let you answer the dog n' bone then, eh?

FLORENCE

Yeah.

ALF SMILES AT HER AS THE DOOR
CLOSES. HE LOOKS AT BERT.

ALF

Credit to the family she is.

BERT

Is she? Litvinoff get her the job did he?

ALF

Yeah, I told him our Florence was looking for a job and Bob's yer uncle.
She's gonna go places she is. There's no flies on our Florence, no. She's
special.

BERT

Special is she?

ALF

I don't mean she's simple. No, she's not simple. There's no simpletons in
our family. She's not got special needs.

BERT

No?

ALF

No. She don't *need* anything. The world's her oyster, mark my words.
She's no mug.

BERT

I never knew you had a niece 'til the other night.

ALF

Oh yeah, nieces, nephews, allsorts.

BERT

Good for you.

ALF

Yeah, I'm lucky.

BERT

Well done.

ALF

Thank you ... anyway, *where was I?*

BERT

When?

ALF

Just then. I was on about summink weren't I?

BERT

Lionel?

ALF

Oh yeah, so I says t' Lionel, I says, "Lionel, yer talkin' out yer hairy bumhole. Rothman was never there. *Rothman* was down Canvey Island up the arcade that day."

ALF SHAKES HIS HEAD AND SNIGGERS.
BERT LOOKS ABOUT, PICKS UP A
PHOTOGRAPHIC CAMERA AND INSPECTS
IT.

BERT

(beat)

These cameras ain't cheap ... German or summink.

ALF

It's Lionel's memory see. Once that's gone ... well ... you can forget about everythin' else once yer memory's gone.

BERT DOESN'T RESPOND, CONTINUES
INSPECTING.

ALF

Don't forget to look after yer memory. You'll thank me when you get older.

BERT

I won't.

BERT PUTS THE CAMERA DOWN AND MOVES ON TO MORE EQUIPMENT.

BERT
(shaking his head, whistles
in admiration re: the
equipment)
There's some loot in here, Alf. It's top notch gear. This is spiffin' equipment this is.

ALF
(shaking his head mournfully)
They'll be carting him off to the funny farm if he carries on not remembering.

BERT

Who?

ALF

Whatshisname.

BERT

Lionel?

ALF

Yeah, Lionel.

BERT

He's up that Dolphin Square ain't he?

ALF

Is he?

BERT

It's what *I* heard.

ALF

(thinks about it)

Mmm ... it don't surprise me. There's a lot o' queer stuff going on up that place down Dolphin Square.

BERT

(beat)

What was that smelly pornographer ratbag down Berwick Street called? You know who I mean. *French* ... Claude or summink.

ALF

Claude? *French Claude?*

BERT

Is that him?

ALF

Yeah, probably. If he was foreign it was probably French Claude.

BERT

Me n' Cyril called on him once. This frog owed Ralph summink. He had all this gear but this gear *in here*. Well, I'm sayin' you wouldn't use *this* gear for a titty flick. It'd be wasted on a wank picture.

THEY KICK THEIR HEELS A LITTLE
MORE.

ALF

Can I have a look at your Mirror?

> BERT

Where's yours?

> ALF

I didn't pick mine up this morning.

> BERT
> (sighing)

I haven't had a look in it yet.

> ALF

I won't it spoil for ya.

> BERT PULLS OUT A NEWSPAPER FROM HIS
> BACK POCKET. ALF SITS DOWN AND
> STARTS TO READ IT FROM THE SPORTING
> PAGES.

> BERT
> (beat)

Litvinoff still coming then?

> ALF
> (beat, re: the sporting
> pages)

... I'm havin' a few bob on Coffee Toffee at Chepstow. It's a dead cert.
> (beat, putting paper down
> momentarily, laughs)

Here, you hear about Freddy having whatshisname on?

> BERT

Who?

> ALF

Freddy.

BERT

I know who Freddy is! We're like brothers. I'd take a bullet for him.
Who'd he have on?

ALF

Him with the white Jag. You know who I mean. Mouthy.

BERT

Nah.

ALF

White Jag. Drinks in The Roebuck. You know him. He's got a mouth on him.

BERT

I don't know who you mean.

ALF

Course ya do. It's on the tip o' me tongue.

ALF CLICKS HIS FINGERS IMPATIENTLY.
BERT WAITS FOR HIM TO REMEMBER.

ALF

He was havin' it off with that blonde sort.
Her with the big Bristol's behind the bar.
Mary or Linda or Trisha or summink.
Wears a leather mini skirt.

BERT

Can't picture him.

ALF

Course you can! You know who I mean! White Jag.
(muttering to himself,
clicking his fingers)
What's his bleedin' name. It'll come to me.

BERT

I don't know him.

ALF
(insistent)

You do! White jag. Wears a cravat. Carry's a walking stick.

BERT

Oh, yeah, brass tipped job?

ALF

That's him! Well Freddy tells him he's got a dead cert. You know what Freddy's like. He tells him it's called *Norfolk Enchants* don't he. He's a bleedin' card he is.

ALF LAUGHS AND WAITS FOR BERT TO
JOIN IN. BERT DOESN'T.

ALF

You hear me, Bert? *Norfolk Enchants.* Norfolk Enchants.

BERT

I've heard it before. It don't tickle me.

ALF
(huffs and then back to the
newspaper)

Well *I* thought it were funny.

BERT

It *is* funny, it's a funny joke, I'm not disputin' the fact. I like jokes that're funny ... I've just heard it before.

BERT CONTINUES HIS INSPECTION OF
THE EQUIPMENT.

ALF

(beat)

Yeah, Coffee Toffee at Chepstow. 3.30. 3 to 1 ... do you reckon our Florence has forgot about that tea? I'm parched I am.

BERT

I'm not touching the horses anymore.

ALF LOWERS THE NEWSPAPER AND FROWNS AT BERT IN SURPRISE.

ALF

But you love a little flutter, Bert!

BERT

You don't need to tell *me* I love a little flutter ... not anymore though.

ALF

(smirking)

Do me a favour. Not touching the nags? Don't talk --

BERT

-- I'm not touching the dogs either. I'm restricting my gambling to the casino aren't I. I'm turning over a new leaf.

ALF

But --

BERT

-- when was the last time you picked up a bird at the dogs?

ALF

(thinks about it)

Huh ... never as a matter o' fact. I've *never* pulled a bird at the dogs.

BERT

There ya go. Ya just answered my question. I'm not spunking it up the dogs n' horses anymore ... you ever see me spunking it up the dogs you got permission to gimme a good clump.

ALF WAVES HIS HAND AT BERT ...

ALF

Codswallop! I've heard it all before.

ALF CARRIES ON READING, BERT PUTS HIS HANDS IN HIS TROUSER POCKETS, STARTS KICKING HIS HEELS IMPATIENTLY.

BERT

What time's Litvinoff getting here? ... he's late.

ALF

What time did he say the other night?

BERT

When? The other night in the boozer?

ALF

Yeah. He was with our Florence wasn't he?

BERT DOESN'T REPLY, SIMPLY CHECKS HIS WATCH.

ALF

You gave her a lift home, eh?

BERT

Who? Me? Did I?

ALF

Yeah.

BERT

I can't remember giving her a lift home. I was paralytic and it were pissing it down. I was all *over* the road.

ALF

It were good of you driving her home. Her old Mum worries about her in the West End of an evening. It's no place for a sixteen year old gallivanting of a night.

BERT

Nah.

ALF

Too many degenerates for my liking.

BERT

They should be strung up n' shot. Drawn n' quartered.

ALF

I don't know what the world's coming to.

BERT
(cutting in over ALF)
You know they got Bindon involved in this lark, eh?

ALF

Have they? Bindon, eh? I like John.

BERT

I dunno ... he's all right I suppose.

ALF

You not fond of him then?

BERT

Fond? Yeah, he's all right … it's wearing a bit thin though, eh? You know. Him n' his knob. Lobbing his old man out all the time. I mean, everyone's got a cock. I don't see why he's gotta flash *his* all over the shop.

ALF

(giggling)

He's hysterical he is. That's his thing.

BERT WAGS HIS FINGER AT ALF.

BERT

You won't catch *me* throwing my Hampton about like that!

ALF

He's proud of his old chap that's all. It's just a giggle.

BERT

I like him, he's stand-up, don't get me wrong, Alf … saw him wrap a roulette wheel round some berk's head down that casino in Battersea once.

ALF THINKS ABOUT IT AND LOOKS UP.

ALF

Wait a minute. I forgot about that … yeah he did didn't he.

BERT

How'd you forget about it when ya weren't even there?

ALF

Eh?

BERT

You weren't there.

ALF

I remember hearing about it, I know *I* weren't there, someone told me
about it I think.

BERT
(pointing at himself)
Yeah, muggings here! Me! I told ya about it.

ALF LAUGHS AND RETURNS TO THE
NEWSPAPER.

ALF

He's a rascal he is ... this bloke asking for it was he?

BERT

Eh?

ALF

The bloke he clobbered. Asking t' get walloped with the roulette wheel
was he?

BERT

Yeah, course he was.

ALF

Well if he was askin' for it, it serves him right. Bindon wouldn't just wrap a
roulette wheel 'round his head if he weren't asking for it.

BERT PACES, FINGERS EQUIPMENT. ALF
LAUGHS AT SOMETHING HE'S READ. BERT
GLANCES AT ALF AND SIGHS IN
DISAPPROVAL.

BERT

Summink funny in *my* mirror?

FLORENCE NERVOUSLY ENTERS WITH A
TEA TRAY: POT, CUPS, MILK, SUGAR,
BISCUITS. SHE'S APOLOGETIC. ALF
STANDS UP.

FLORENCE

I had to answer a phone call, sorry.

ALF
(proud)

You answered a phone call, eh? You hear that, Bert? *She answered a phone
call.* It's only yesterday she was fillin' her nappies on me knees. Look at
her, sweet sixteen. I never thought I'd see the day.

BERT WATCHES FLORENCE CLOSELY AS
SHE PUTS THE TRAY DOWN. SHE CATCHES
HIM STARING AND AVERTS HER GAZE.

FLORENCE

Do you want me to pour or can you do it?

ALF

I can do it, you've done more than enough, petal.

FLORENCE

I'll only be next door if you need me. I'm not going anywhere.

BERT
(cold)

We're all right. Alf can pour. We won't *need* you.

ALF

Here, Florence, tell Bert about that thing you won.

FLORENCE

What thing, Uncle?

ALF

The thing from that place you used to go.

FLORENCE

Huh ... I can't think.

ALF

You know, Girl Cubs or summink.

FLORENCE

Girl Cubs?

ALF

Yeah, you used to dress up. Church Hall up the end of Roper Street next door to the bomb site.

FLORENCE

I can't remember.

FLORENCE THINKS, SHE'S CLEARLY MORE EMBARRASSED.

ALF

We was all over the moon. We had a knees up.

FLORENCE

Huh, you don't mean ... you don't mean when I was in The Brownies do ya?

ALF

That's it, you used to wear a uniform. Brown shirt, blouse, whatever. You looked handsome.

FLORENCE GIGGLES NERVOUSLY.

FLORENCE

I was only eight, Uncle. Give over.

ALF

We was all made up. She won a badge, Bert.

BERT
(unimpressed)

Did she?

FLORENCE

It was nothing, *everyone* got one. It didn't mean nothing.

ALF

She's being modest, Bert. She's just like her Old Mum.

FLORENCE

No, Uncle, honest. It was nothing.

ALF

Her Old Mum's the same. Runs in the family.

FLORENCE

I better get back.

ALF

Your Old Man showed that badge to everyone.

FLORENCE

It was just a badge from The Brownies.

ALF

Meant the world to him. He was choked up with pride he was. Brought a tear to his eye that badge did.

FLORENCE LEAVES AND ALF POURS THE TEA.

ALF

Spittin' image of her Old Mum. Modest.

BERT

Is she?

ALF

Oh yeah ...
(beat)
I'm partial to a good cup o' rosy ... I always get a ragin' thirst when I've been drinkin'.

BERT

Me too. Everyone does.

ALF

I always end up parched after a drink.

BERT

I know.

ALF

I bumped in to some o' me old mates from the print down The Yacht Club last night ... haven't seen 'em in donkeys years ... they're getting older now.

BERT

Are they?

ALF
(savoring the tea)

Aaaahhh, that's a lovely cuppa that is. Our Florence has done us proud
again ... she'll go far she will.

BERT

She, huh, she looks older than sixteen.

ALF

That's the fashion nowadays innit. Young un's wanna look old
and old bints wanna look like young un's. It's all topsy turvy. *It's
iggle-di-bleedin'-piggle-dy.*

BERT
(quietly)

They shouldn't mess about with their ages.

ALF GIGGLES AS HE REMEMBERS
SOMETHING.

ALF

You know what my old Dad says about dolly birds don't ya?

BERT

Your old Dad's dead ain't he? How would *I* know what he says?

ALF

When he was alive.

BERT

I've only known him dead. I met you when he'd kicked the bucket
didn't I?

ALF THINKS ABOUT IT AND THEN SLOWLY
NODS HIS HEAD.

ALF

You'd o' liked my Old Man. He was a Docker.

BERT

Everyone was a Docker in them days.

ALF

I know ... I looked up to my Old Man. There was nothing wrong with working down The Docks.

BERT

I know. Everyone was a Docker.

ALF

He was a proud man. Immaculate. Always wore a whistle when he weren't down The Docks.

ALF LOOKS INTO THE DISTANCE,
CLEARLY THINKING ABOUT HIS FATHER.

ALF

We buried him in his best whistle. He'd o' liked that. We did him proud ... he wanted to be cremated but my Old Mum wasn't having any of it. I don't reckon he'd o' kicked up a stink about *not* being buried though.

BERT

No.

ALF

He loved my Old Mum.

BERT

Did he?

ALF

Oh yeah, definitely. He never showed it but you could tell.

BERT
(beat)
Here, what do you reckon all this gear's worth?

ALF
(suspiciously)
What you thinking? You're thinking summink you are. You got summink on your mind you have. You're thinking.

BERT
(defensive)
No I ain't! I ain't thinkin' anythin'. What makes you think that?

ALF LOWERS HIS VOICE. STARTS
POURING MORE TEA.

ALF
We can't have this place over, Bert.

BERT
Who said anything about *having it over*?

ALF
You did.

BERT
No I didn't! When?

ALF
Yes you did! Just then! That ... that *tone*.

BERT
(snorts)
What bleedin' tone? I ain't got a *tone*.
(beat)
And anyway, never mind my tone, where's Litvinoff?

ALF

He's not here.

BERT

I know he's not. Where is he then? Why's he late? Why's he got us waiting
here like a pair o' prats, eh?

ALF SHRUGS AND MAKES A MOTION
SUGGESTING WHETHER HE SHOULD POUR
BERT ANOTHER CUPPA. BERT MOTIONS
FOR HIM NOT TO.

ALF

How do we know he's late for a start? For a start: what time did he say?
How do you know it's us that's not early?

BERT

Cos I'm never early am I. What's the point o' that! You turn up
somewhere early n' there's never nobody there!

ALF SIPS HIS TEA AND THINKS ABOUT
IT. BERT SWILLS HIS CUP AND STARES
AT THE LEAVES IN THE BOTTOM OF IT.
FLORENCE POPS HER HEAD AROUND THE
DOOR. SHE'S STILL A LITTLE NERVOUS,
NEVER MAKING EYE CONTACT WITH BERT.

FLORENCE

Mmm, Donald's just rung up, Uncle Alf. He's really sorry but he's stuck
in a meeting with Mr. Jagger. He's gonna be late.

BERT
(cold)

Who's this *Donald?*

FLORENCE

Huh, Mr. Cammell.

BERT

Never heard of him. Who's he when he's at home?

FLORENCE

He's, huh ... he's who you're meeting.

BERT

Where is he then? *We're* here! Me and yer Uncle Alf are here. Where's he, Florrie?

FLORENCE

He said to apologize. He doesn't usually get tied up.

BERT

Why's he tied up *now* then?

FLORENCE

Cos he's with Mr. Jagger.

ALF
(diffusing)
Oh he should o' told us he'd be tied up, we could o' popped in later.

FLORENCE

Mmm, that's why he telephoned me.

ALF
(shooting a glare at BERT
over his attitude, putting
his hand on FLORENCE'S arm)
Tell him it's all right, precious. Thanks for telling us.

BERT
(a little contrite)
Huh, yeah, sorry, I huh, I didn't mean to sound -- sorry Florrie.

FLORENCE
-- s' all right.

ALF
You're doing a lovely job, Florence. Everyone's dead proud.

FLORENCE
Stop it, Uncle.

ALF
You're modest you are.

FLORENCE
I'm not, Uncle, stop it.

ALF
You're a dead ringer for your Old Mum.

FLORENCE
I've got to ...

FLORENCE BACKS OUT, CLEARLY A
LITTLE EMBARRASSED.

BERT
I didn't mean to snap at her, Alf.

ALF
She's good as gold she is. Apple of her Dad's eye ... she must like *you*.

BERT
(bristles, defensive)
Eh? What's that supposed to mean. What do you mean by that?

ALF

Letting you call her "Florrie". She hates us calling her Florrie or Flo.

BERT IS CLEARLY NOW EVEN MORE
UNCOMFORTABLE AND TRIES TO MASK IT.

BERT

Oh I, huh, I call everyone Florrie ... I mean, everyone who's called Florrie like.

ALF LOOKS AT SOME FILM REELS,
LIFTS ONE UP AND SNORTS ...

ALF

Look at this. It says 'Kenneth Anger'.

BERT

What sort o' name's that? That's a moody name if ever I heard one. No cunt's called 'Anger'

ALF

It's what you call a coincidence is what it is.

BERT

What's *what* you call a coincidence?

ALF

"Kenneth". *Kenneth*, Kenny, our Florence's Dad.

BERT FROWNS.

BERT

Her Dad's Teddy ain't he?

ALF

No, she's Kenneth's. She's not Ted's.

BERT IS SHOCKED, BUT MASKS IT.

ALF

Teddy's kids ain't girls.

BERT

No? What are they then?

ALF

They're boys. He's got Little Ted and thingy, the other one.

BERT

So ... so she's -- Florence is Kenny's eh?

ALF

Yeah, Teddy's got two boys. He ain't got nothing against little girls, he just prefers little boys.

BERT

I didn't know.

ALF

He don't make a big thing of it.

BERT

No, I mean that Florence is Kenny's.

ALF

Oh yeah. Definitely. There's no question about it.

FLORENCE POPS HER HEAD AROUND THE
DOOR. BERT RUBS AT HIS COLLAR AND
PACES.

ALF

Speak o' the devil. We was just talking about you, Florence.

FLORENCE

Crispin's coming in, Uncle.

ALF

Oh is he? Good ... who's Crispin?

FLORENCE

He works for Mr. Cammel. He's coming in.

ALF

Telephone you did he?

FLORENCE

Yeah, he telephoned.

ALF

Good for him. Bert here thought your Old Man was your Uncle Ted.

FLORENCE

Oh, did he?

ALF

Yeah he did. You thought her Old Man was Teddy didn't you, Bert?
(to Florence)
I told him, I said, "No you berk, our Florence is our Kenny's daughter." I said, "Our Teddy's got boys. He hasn't got girls."

FLORENCE

Huh, yeah. They're boys.

ALF

That's right. They're your cousins.

FLORENCE

I know.

FLORENCE WAITS FOR BERT TO
RESPOND. HE DOESN'T AND FLORENCE
POPS BACK OUT OF THE DOOR.

FLORENCE

Well ... Crispin'll be here soon.

ALF

Thanks for telling us, treacle.

BERT

(a little nervous)

Your Kenny still inside is he?

ALF

He's out The Scrubs end o' June.

BERT

I bet he's done his porridge standing on his head, eh?

ALF

Water off a duck's back. He could do six years porridge in his sleep he
could. He can do bird standing on his head. He's a natural.

BERT

I've always liked him. Got a lot of respect for him I have.

ALF

Everyone has. He's *stand-up*. Always has been. You ever see him go toe t'
toe on the cobbles?

(chuckles)

When he took on Wilf Nash n' his brothers. *Jesus!* Hospitalized the lot
of 'em. Had their guts for garters. Plastered 'em all over Poland Street.
Marmalized 'em he did.

ALF MUSES AND STARTS TO PLAYFULLY
SHADOW BOX. BERT SITS DOWN AND
STARES AT HIS WATCH.

BERT
(beat)
Crispin? Camel? Anger? You'd change yer bleedin' name if you was called that wouldn't ya?

ALF
You know what these showbiz types are like. More than likely foreign. Probably a moody name.

BERT
Imagine calling yerself after a camel though. They're dirty little bleeders. Always spittin'. I seen one in a zoo once.
Come to think of it he was eyeballin' me the cheeky cunt, just starin' ... they should be shot ... vermin.

ALF SITS DOWN AND PICKS UP THE
NEWSPAPER.

BERT
And Mick Jagger. Jesus! He gets right on my tits he does. He's never off the Hit Parade, never off the bleedin' telly. He's a queer little twerp he is. If you ask me there's something not right about him. I don't see the attraction.

ALF
Old rubber lips. Yeah, Litvinoff said he's in this picture. They never done nothin' for me. You know what *I* like? I like that song, *"Love Is Everything"*. That's what you call a song.

BERT
I don't know it.

ALF
Course you do.

                        BERT

Nah, I don't think so.

                        ALF

Course you do! Give over.

          ALF STARTS TO WHISTLE THE MELODY.

                        BERT

Nah, never heard of it, can't picture it

                        ALF

'S on the radio all the time. You'd have to be deaf not to hear it.

                        BERT

I only listen to the horses on the radio.

          ALF CLOSES IN ON BERT AND WHISTLES
          THE MELODY MORE FORCEFULLY, FASTER.
          BERT SHAKES HIS HEAD NEGATIVE.

                        BERT

Nah, you've lost me.

                        ALF

But *everyone's* bleedin' heard it, Bert!

                        BERT

You sure it's not called summink else?

                        ALF

I'm not making it up!

                        BERT

I didn't say you was.

ALF

Well I'm not ... I don't make songs up! They don't call me *Burt* bleedin'
Baccaract (sic), Bert!

BERT

(snapping)

If I'd heard it I'd know it but I just can't picture it.

BERT PULLS A BRASS KNUCKLE DUSTER
OUT OF HIS SUIT JACKET INSIDE
POCKET. HE SLIPS IT ON AND STARTS
TO PUNCH HIS PALM WITH IT AND PACES
ABOUT. AFTER A WHILE ALF NOTICES.

ALF

What you doing wi' that knuckle?

BERT

Nothin'.

(re: the knuckle duster)

What? This?

ALF

Why you brought a duster, Bert? This is a meeting.

BERT

(snorts)

"Meeting" he says! You need *people* to have a meeting. There's no pillock
here. It's like a morgue in here, like a ghost train at the seaside or
summink.

ALF

We're meeting a picture person. He's late that's all. He's got tied up with a
Rolling Stone ... why you getting airyated?

BERT
(defensive)
I'm *not* getting airyated! Who said I'm getting airyated?

ALF GIVES BERT A LOOK AND SIGHS.

ALF
You got the hump you have.

ALF SNAPS THE NEWSPAPER STRAIGHT AND READS.
BERT CONTINUES PUNCHING HIS PALM AND PACING.

BERT
(under his breath, snorts)
Mick Jagger. Who's he think he is ... bleedin' *ponce*.

ALF
Eh? What you rabbiting on about?

BERT
If *I* say I'm meeting someone I expect 'em to turn up ... it's common
courtesy ... you just imagine if nobody ever turned up to meetings. You'd
have a right palaver you would. It'd be anarchy, there'd be murders.

ALF SIGHS, FOLDS THE NEWSPAPER,
PUTS IT DOWN AND CROSSES HIS LEGS.

ALF
Have you got somewhere else to be or what, Bert?

BERT
Me? ... somewhere to go? How d'ya mean?

ALF
That why yer getting airyated is it?

BERT

If ya must know I'm gonna nip over Brick Lane later. I'm gonna have a word with Mitch.

ALF

Mitch, eh? *Which* Mitch?

BERT

Mitch with the eyes.

ALF

Not Mitch up Golders Green with the launderettes?

BERT

Nah, that's the other Mitch. You know, *Mitch with the eyes.*

ALF
(momentarily pauses)
Maurice's brother?

BERT

His brother's called Solly last I heard.

ALF

I thought it were Maurice?
(frowns, to himself)
Why'd I think he was called Maurice? I'm usually good with names.

BERT

His brother's always been called Solly far as I know.

ALF

Oh yeah, yeah, so it is ... I know who you mean now.

BERT SLIPS THE KNUCKLE DUSTER
BACK IN HIS POCKET.

                    ALF

What's he done?

                    BERT

Who? Mitch?

                    ALF

Yeah, you gonna spank his arse, eh? Been a naughty boy as he?

                    BERT

As it happens he has ... he owes someone a few quid.

                    ALF
              (putting his hand up in mock
                    surrender)
Don't tell me, I don't wanna know. None o' my business.

                    BERT

It's Clive if ya must know. He owes Clive a monkey.

                    ALF
              (tutting, shaking his head)
Borrowed a monkey from Clive did he? What a prat!
                (beat, he ponders and
                then clicks his fingers)
One of his kids' got that spina bifida.

                    BERT

Who? One o' Mitch's kids?

                    ALF

Yeah, yeah. Terrible disease. There was a charity snooker match. Lovely
spread. They raised a few bob and sent her off to Brighton or summink ...
come to think of it I've not seen her since they sent her off ... I hope she's not
dead.

BERT

He should o' thought about Brighton and snooker n' spina bifida when he was borrowing a monkey off Clive and not giving it back.

ALF

(reflective)

I don't know how *I'd* feel if my teapot had that spina bifida ... I wouldn't be too happy that's f'sure.

BERT

You ain't got a kid.

ALF

N' I don't want one if they've got spina bifida thank you very much!

ALF STANDS UP AND STRAIGHTENS HIS CLOTHES.

ALF

(rubbing his hands together)

Right. I'm nipping downstairs to the Bookies. I'm gonna have a few bob on *Coffee Toffee* at Chepstow.

BERT

How long you gonna be? Don't be long.

ALF

It's only downstairs. Two ticks.

BERT

Don't be all day then. I'm not waitin' here on me todd for this bleedin' camel to turn up.

ALF GOES TO THE DOOR AND HEADS OUT.

ALF

I'll be back before you know it.

BERT PACES. HE STOPS AND SIGHS AND
STARTS TO EXAMINE A SUPER 8 CAMERA.
FLORENCE SHEEPISHLY ENTERS AND LEAVES
THE DOOR SLIGHTLY AJAR. BERT GROANS WHEN
HE SEES HER BUT MUSTERS UP A SMILE.

BERT

You never said your Dad was Kenny.

FLORENCE

Didn't I? I can't remember ... Uncle Ted's my Uncle. They look alike but
he's not my Dad.

BERT TURNS HIS BACK ON HER.

FLORENCE

Huh ... can I ... can I talk to you?

FLORENCE HAS HER HEAD BOWED. BOTH
ARE CLEARLY EMBARRASSED.

BERT

It's a small world, eh? I'm sayin'... I didn't know we'd be here together.

FLORENCE

I thought I told ya the other night ... I thought I said.

BERT

I probably wasn't listening.

FLORENCE

Probably ... it was loud in there.

BERT

Yeah, not that I can remember though. I'd been drinking all day. I was steamin' I was.

FLORENCE

Yeah, you was drinking at the time.

BERT

Yeah, I will have been. I always have a drink when I'm in the boozer.
(beat, floundering for
something to say)
I, huh, I knew someone who worked in an office once.

FLORENCE

Did ya?

BERT

Oh yeah ... it were down Shaftesbury Avenue I think.

FLORENCE

Was it? ... that's nice. There's a lot of offices down there.

BERT

Yeah, huh ... it's a busy street Shaftesbury Avenue.

FLORENCE

I know. My friend works in a shoe shop down Shaftesbury Avenue.

BERT

Does she?

FLORENCE

Yeah ... she was in my class at school.

BERT

A shoe shop, eh?

FLORENCE

Freeman Hardy n' Willis.

BERT

Right. Not Clarks then?

FLORENCE

No. Freeman Hardy n' Willis.

BERT

I get me shoes down Savile Row. You can't skimp on shoes.

FLORENCE

No.

BERT

They've gotta fit right see. You don't wanna be wearing shoes that don't fit. Oh yeah, you could do yourself a mischief you could.

FLORENCE

Bunions and things.

BERT

Athletes Foot. All sorts. You could cripple yourself you ain't careful.

FLORENCE

My Nan's got bunions.

BERT

Has she? ... the old sage n' onions, eh?
(tutting)
.. yeah, you see, she probably wore shoes that didn't fit when she was a teapot. You should tell her to wear shoes that fit.

FLORENCE

She won't listen. She's a bit stubborn.

BERT

Is she? Bless her, don't like being told what t' do, eh?

FLORENCE

No. She's like that.

BERT

Old is she? Your Nan knocking on, eh?

FLORENCE

Yeah.

BERT

Yeah, I thought so ... old people don't like being told what t' do see. It's cos o' the war. Rationing n' all that. The Blitz.

FLORENCE

Yeah.
                    (beat)
I, mmm, can we ... I wanted to --

BERT
                    (quietly, rushing)
-- that *thing* the other night ... that fumble, all that muckin' about. We, huh ... well, we shouldn't have done it lookin' back ... I, huh ... I thought you was older truth be told.

FLORENCE

I told you how young I was. I said I wasn't old.

BERT

Yeah, but I was drivin' n' I'd been drinkin' n' I never pay attention when I'm in that state ... I was paralytic. I mean, underneath all that make-up ... all that slapstick, well ... I mean, ya could be as old as my Old Mum far as I know. It's the fashion innit.

FLORENCE
(meekly)

I've been worried.

BERT

Worried? What *you* worried about? You got the whole world at yer feet ... you do a lovely cup o' tea.

FLORENCE
(beat)

I ... I couldn't ... I haven't been able to get to sleep proper.

BERT

You ain't told anyone have ya?

FLORENCE

About not sleeping proper?

BERT

No, no ... the, huh ... the bit o' frolicking. The hanky panky.

FLORENCE
(shaking her head)

No, no ... course not. I wouldn't dare and I'm not that type o' girl. It was ... well, it was the first time I've ... I'm not like some girls. I know some girls that do things but I'm not one of 'em. I never do things like that.

BERT

So you ain't told nobody then?

FLORENCE

No. Nobody. I'm not like that.

BERT

Your Old Dad wouldn't be happy would he? He'd be happy you didn't tell no one. He wouldn't want people thinking his Daughter was like that, eh?

FLORENCE

No, God! I'd *never* tell him! He'd kill me. He's got a really bad temper.

BERT

You're a clever girl you are. You know what's good for you.

FLORENCE

I've not been brought up to grass n' besides, I'd never grass *myself* up.

BERT

Nobody likes a grass. You know which side your bread's buttered you do.

BERT SIGHS IN RELIEF AND PACES.
HE TURNS AND LOOKS AT HER.

FLORENCE

I never drink really ... it were those Babycham. I was a bit tipsy. I mean, I'd never usually ... I'm not like that.

BERT

It's all right, you don't have to apologize ... and look, you've nothing to worry about if you ain't told nobody. There's only me n' you knows about it n' we'd be round the bleedin' twist if we said somethin' over a bit of o' slap n' tickle. And you're right, yer Old Man'd kill ya n' I wouldn't wanna see that happen, Florence. It'd be a shame.

FLORENCE

I'm never gonna say anything. I'm not stupid.

BERT

I know, I know, you couldn't work in an office if you was stupid.

FLORENCE

I just wanna forget about it.

BERT

Everyone wants to forget about it. It's not something anyone wants to remember.

FLORENCE

I don't remember half of it anyway.

BERT

Me neither. I don't remember *any* of it. I'm just taking your word for it to be honest.

FLORENCE

I'm never drinking Babycham again.

BERT

You shouldn't. It's not good for ya. You should stick to pop. Stick to Dandelion n' Burdock. There's nothing wrong with a nice Dandelion n' Burdock.

FLORENCE

I only like Dandelion n' Burdock with fish n' chips.

BERT

Well, huh, lemonade then. Or a shandy. I bet you like a lager n' lime, eh?

FLORENCE

Yeah, it's nice.

BERT

Yeah, women like lager n' lime. Or lager n' black.

FLORENCE

Yeah, me Mum likes lager n' black.

BERT

I thought she might ...

BERT CLOSES IN ON HER.

BERT

Listen, look, uh, yer Uncle Alf's only nipped out for a minute. It's best we don't talk about things in here.

BERT PULLS OUT HIS WALLET AND TAKES OUT A FIVE POUND NOTE. HE FORCES IT INTO FLORENCE'S HAND. SHE FROWNS AT HIM.

BERT

Here, I insist. It's a fiver. Buy yerself summink nice.

FLORENCE

I don't ... no thanks.

BERT

Treat yerself. Go on. Have a blowout on me. You've earned it.

FLORENCE HOLDS THE FIVE POUND NOTE OUT TO BERT. HE GRABS HER HAND AND CLOSES IT TIGHT.

BERT

Keep it. Buy summink nice. I want ya to have it ... you make a lovely cup o' rosy you do.

FLORENCE

Did you ... I mean ... you didn't...

BERT

What?

FLORENCE

The other night ... you didn't ...

BERT IMPATIENTLY CLOSES IN FURTHER.

BERT
(rubbing the back of his
neck)
Spit it out, love. We shouldn't be talkin', just spit it out.

FLORENCE

You know when you ... when you...

BERT

When I what?

FLORENCE

When you ...
(beat)
I dunno how to say it.

BERT

That don't matter. Just say it.
(beat)
Spit it out.

FLORENCE
(beat)
When you ... when ya finished.

BERT

Finished? No, you've lost me.

FLORENCE
(even quieter)
When ya ... after we'd ... when ya come.

                        BERT

Eh? Oh, right, right. When I ...

                      FLORENCE

Yeah.

                        BERT

Right, huh ... what about it?

                      FLORENCE

I ... I don't like to say. I'm not that sort of girl. It were the Babycham.

                        BERT

S'alright, just say it.

                      FLORENCE

Did you ... you know ... did ya do it inside?

            BERT SIGHS IN RELIEF AGAIN AND
            SMILES AT FLORENCE.

                        BERT

Aaahhh, right. You was worried I'd shot me muck up ya, ya silly sausage.

            HE PATS HER ON THE HEAD. FLORENCE
            FROWNS AT HIM.

                        BERT

You got nothing to worry about. I was wearing a Rubber Johnny weren't
I. I *always* wear a Rubber Johnny. I never leave home without a Rubber
Johnny. You don't have to worry about havin' a bun in the oven. Just buy
yerself summink nice with that Lady Godiva n' forget it ever happened. It
were just a bit of 'How's yer father' that went too far that's all.
                        (beat)
N' I gotta be honest. You wouldn't have had to worry at all if you'd let me
do what I asked.

FLORENCE
(cringing)
You mean ... you mean up my ...

BERT
It's all the rage nowadays. Everyone's doin' it up the bum. It don't mean you're a poof if you do it up the bum with a bird.

FLORENCE
(shudders)
I can't even think about it. It's not right. It's dirty.

BERT
Look, just take the fiver and treat yourself.

FLORENCE PAUSES AND STARES AT THE FIVER.

FLORENCE
(beat)
It's not a lot is it?

BERT
Eh?

FLORENCE
A fiver. I mean ... it's not a lot.

BERT
It's enough to get yerself summink handsome.

FLORENCE LOOKS UP AND STARES HIM IN THE EYES. AFTER A WHILE BERT SIGHS, REALIZING HER GAME.

                    BERT

How much were you thinkin'?

                    FLORENCE
                 (shrugging)

I dunno.

                    BERT

What about a tenner?

          FLORENCE CONTINUES STARING.

                    BERT

What? A Score?

          FLORENCE SHRUGS AND LOOKS AWAY.

                    BERT

A Pony then? What about a Pony? I'm only holding a Pony.

                    FLORENCE
                  (beat)

I was thinking ... well ... what about fifty?

                    BERT

Fifty!

                    FLORENCE

No, no. It's OK ...
                 (leaving)
... I was thinking it'd be nice to throw my Dad a party when he gets out
The Scrubs.

                    BERT

Wait a minute, I --

FLORENCE

-- no, it's all right. I understand.

BERT

No, no, here. You're right.

FLORENCE

I don't wanna look like ... it'd be nice surprise for him though.

BERT COUNTS OUT FIFTY POUND NOTES
FROM HIS MONEY CLIP AND QUICKLY
HANDS THEM TO HER.

FLORENCE

You sure?

BERT
(hiding his anger)

Just take it.

FLORENCE

All right then. If you insist.

FLORENCE PUTS THE CASH IN HER
SKIRT. BERT IS FUMING BUT CLEARLY
RELIEVED AS WELL.

FLORENCE

I'll make sure Uncle Alf invites you to the party.

SUDDENLY ALF ENTERS AND FLORENCE
QUICKLY STARTS TO COLLECT THE
CUPS AND SAUCERS AND THE TEAPOT.

ALF
(looking around)

That Camel and thingummie not here yet then? Have I missed anything?

BERT
(hurried)
Nothin'. You put yer bet on then, eh?

ALF
Three sov's each way, dead cert. What have I missed?

FLORENCE
(avoiding eye contact with
ALF)
Nothin', Uncle. I'm just tidying this tea away.

ALF
That was a blindin' cuppa, Florence, even if I say so myself.

FLORENCE
Thanks Uncle.

ALF
You're welcome.

ALF WATCHES HER. SHE STARTS TO
HEAD OUT. HE STOPS HER.

ALF
(to BERT)
Tell Florence what I said about her cuppa?

BERT
He, huh, he said it was the best cup o' tea he's ever had.

FLORENCE SMILES AT ALF AND HE
LETS HER PASS, PATTING HER ON THE
BACK AS SHE GOES. ALF STARTS
PACING. BERT LEANS BACK ON A
TABLE, TRYING TO COMPOSE HIMSELF.

ALF

I'll probably go for a quick drink when we've finished here. I might nip in and see old Bernard, see if his lumbago's any better ... I wonder if this Camel likes a drink. These showbiz types drink like fish.

BERT

That's a load of old codswallop.

ALF

Eh?

BERT

Fish drinking a lot. A load of old tosh. There's been studies done at universities. They looked into how much fish drink. They don't drink anymore than anyone else as it happens. It's an old fish wives tale.

ALF

Well I ain't gonna argue with no scientists. They're very clever people you know? You don't see any backward scientists. A dummy wouldn't last two minutes in that old science lark.

BERT
(beat)
I bet they don't keep Mick Jagger waitin' like this.

ALF

Who?

BERT

Mick Jagger. Bet they don't have Mick Jagger waitin' on 'em like a pair o' berks.

ALF
(beat)
You've got whatchamacallhim on yer mind ain't ya? Brick Lane.

BERT
I don't like being mugged off that's all.
(turns to ALF)
Shall we fuck off?

ALF
"Fuck off"?

BERT
Let's fuck off. I'm not waitin' here all day.

ALF
We've only been here a minute. You heard our Florence. Not his fault he's
tied up with a Rolling Stone, it could happen to anyone.

BERT
It's not good manners ... you didn't have good manners in our house n'
you got a good clip round the ear.

ALF
Them was different times. That was the past.

BERT
Yeah, I know, I was only a nipper ... still ...

A MEMORY COMES TO ALF AND HE
CHUCKLES.

ALF

Here, I remember givin' my Old Nan some lip once. I was being saucy n' she walloped me with a poker ... nearly took my bleedin' head off with it ... cut me wide open. Still got the scar from the stitches ... still itches... to this day the scar still itches from the stitches n' I always think about her when it does ... I'll never forget her ... never forget that pong.

(looking upwards)

Wonder what she's doing up there, bless her ... probably knitting or playing pontoon. She'll *definitely* be playing bingo, that's fer sure. Loves it she does. *Obsessed.* Like a man possessed when she's playing bingo she is.

BERT

I bet you never got saucy with yer Old Nan after that, eh.

ALF

I was terrified of her ... she was lovely my Old Nan. Every man and woman in the world had a good word for her. I'm not exaggerating.

BERT

That's what ya call respect that is. Not like nowadays. These young un's nowadays, schemin' little baskets.

ALF

Blind as a bat but always had a kind word for everyone. Stunk o' carbolic n' pastry.

BERT

Pen n' ink did she?

ALF

Not half. Summink rotten, bless her.

BERT

I never knew my Old Nan. She was dead before I turned up.

ALF

You'd o' liked her, Albert.

BERT

(frowning)

How did *you* know my Old Nan?

ALF

My Old Nan. Not yours. I never knew *yours* ... no, she was a tiny little thing. Three stone wet through. Survived two World Wars single handed. Gave those bleedin' Krauts a run for their money she did.

BERT

They made 'em different back then.

ALF

They didn't put up with any sauce or lip or cheek.

BERT

(beat)

My old Mum give me a right old clump with a stick once.

ALF

A walking stick, eh?

BERT

Nah, just some old stick that was lying about. It hurt though.

ALF

They do. Stick's don't half hurt you hit someone right. You catch someone right with a stick n' you can do some damage.

                    BERT

I know ... it's what these young un's need. They need a good hiding with
a stick. They want a leathering they do. Hanging's too good for 'em. They
need teaching a lesson.

        BERT VIGOROUSLY SCRATCHES HIS CHIN.

                    BERT
                  (beat)
I dunno. Let's fuck off, Alf.

                    ALF
But we're here now. Give it a minute.

                    BERT
We've give it a minute already.

                    ALF
Give it *another* minute.

                    BERT
          (under his breath, seething)
Fuckin' Litvinoff!

                    ALF
You know what he's like. He's harmless.

                    BERT
He'll be *harmless* when I collar him. He'll be laughin' on the other side of
his boat. I'll give him a right earful when I clap eyes on him. I'll give him
a piece o' my bleedin' mind.

                    ALF
He'll be in the Coach n' Horses.

BERT

I know. Or The French.

ALF

Or The Colony or The Coach n' Horses. He loves it in there ... he's a card.

BERT

He'll be a card when I collar him. *Who's he think he is.*

ALF

They love a good drink his pals. Litvinoff's actin' pals. Always on the piss n' never short of a bob or two. Always got a nice bit o' skirt with 'em as well ... tarts love actors, eh ... I once seen 'em swarmin' 'round that Peter O Toole. Fightin' 'em off he was.

BERT

They're good at talkin' that's why.

ALF

Who? Actors?

BERT

Yeah. They got the gift o' the gab, well known fact ... they just give it a load o' flannel n' the birds fall for it... good f' them I say. You can't blame 'em. We're all men at the end of the day. Nothing wrong with havin' it off. It's natural ... most of 'em are bleedin' pansies though. The scrubbers'll never get a proper seein' to by that mob.

ALF

O Toole's not a poof! He was Lawrence Of Arabia!

BERT

Yer gonna get the odd one that ain't queer. It's Sods Law or summink.

ALF

I dunno. They never struck me as nancy boys. I mean you got yer John Wayne, yer Gary Cooper, yer Rock Hudson ... I'm not having it that Burt Lancaster's a shirtlifter.

BERT

Yeah, no, but *they're* Americans. It's not as rife over there. It's these *English* actors, these toffee nosed twerps. It all starts at these private bleedin' schools they send 'em to. Turns 'em into little bum boys from the off.

ALF

You reckon, eh?

BERT

(counting off on his fingers)
Yer MP's, yer Lords, yer Judges, all at it wi' the young slags down The Dilly. They think it's normal... wouldn't know what t' do with a cunt if it jumped up n' smacked 'em in the mush.

ALF

I don't see the attraction. It baffles *me*.

BERT

(in disgust)
What? Stickin' yer Hampton up someone elses smelly arse?

ALF

It's not right is it?

BERT

What's the attraction, that's what I wanna know. What do they get out of it, eh ... just imagine it.

ALF

I can't imagine it.

BERT

Neither can I ... it's unnatural ... I mean, just imagine it.

BERT IS CLEARLY "IMAGINING" IT.

BERT

(reflective)

Two men, stuck up each others arse ... slobberin' all over each other like animals ... slowly tossing each other off in a public lav ... people watchin'. Egging 'em on ... kissing each other all over the shop. Bold as brass ... proud as ya like ... talkin' filth, sucking each other off.
They love it cos they know at any minute they could get caught ... what's that all about then? Where's the fun in that, Alf?

ALF

Filthy bleeders! They're degenerates if you ask me.

BERT GLANCES AT ALF, AND THEN
SURREPTITIOUSLY ADJUSTS HIS GROIN
AREA. ALF SIGHS AND LOOKS AROUND.
BERT LOOKS DOWN AT HIS FEET AND
STARTS TAPPING THEM. ALF SUDDENLY
REMEMBERS SOMETHING. HIS FACE
LIGHTS UP.

ALF

Here, I never told ya, did I! I just remembered. Guess who was in J Arthur's last night?

BERT

Who?

ALF

Guess?

BERT

Who?

ALF

Guess. You'll never guess.

BERT

(shrugs)

I dunno. It could be anyone.

ALF

Have another guess.

BERT

Englebert Humperdink.

ALF

Don't be daft. *Guess.*

BERT

I dunno! How do *I* know? I weren't there.

ALF

Just bleedin' guess.

BERT

Brigitte Bardot.

ALF

Give over ya silly bleeder.

BERT

Just tell me then!

ALF

Thingymabob. He used to work for Charlie and Eddie. Big cauliflower ears, built like a brick khazi. *You* know who I mean. He reminds me a bit of Henry Cooper.

BERT

How the bleedin' hell do *I* know who reminds *you* of Henry Copper?

THE DOOR SWINGS OPENS. BERT AND
ALF REGARD THE ENTRANCE OF CRISPIN
- SLIM, TALL, LONG HAIR, AFGHAN
COAT, WHITE T – SHIRT, LEATHER
TROUSERS, LEATHER BOOTS, A PAISLEY
SCARF AROUND HIS NECK, CARRYING A
LARGE NOTEBOOK. CRISPIN IS
CONFIDENT AND CLEARLY IN A HURRY.
FLORENCE IS BEHIND HIM.

FLORENCE

This is Crispin who I said was coming.

CRISPIN

You must be David's friends?

ALF
(Offering his hand to shake)
Litvinoff? Yeah. We been waitin' on him but he ain't here.

CRISPIN IGNORES ALF'S OFFER OF A
SHAKE, OPENS THE NOTEBOOK ON THE
TABLE AND FLICKS THROUGH THE
PAGES. ALF LETS THE SNUB SLIDE.
BERT WATCHES CRISPIN, GETTING HIS
MEASURE.

ALF

We reckon Litvinoff's late cos he ain't here ... we're not too sure though. We could be a bit early at the end o' the day.

BERT

No we're not! We're *never* early. We're always on time.

CRISPIN LOOKS OVER AT FLORENCE.

CRISPIN

Do you want something?

FLORENCE

Pardon?

CRISPIN

You can go now.

FLORENCE

Oh, yeah. If you need anything ...

ALF

We'll be all right, petal. She's my brother's Daughter. My niece. A credit to the family she is. She makes a lovely cuppa -- goes to University at night in her spare time.

CRISPIN

Donald's with Mick ... Mick Jagger ... Rolling Stones?

CRISPIN WAITS FOR THEM TO BE IMPRESSED. THEY'RE NOT IMPRESSED.

CRISPIN

Anyway, he's asked me pop in and have a look at you both.

BERT

"Have a look at us"? What does *that* mean?

CRISPIN

To see what you look like.

ALF

Oh, right you are, huh, well ... we're Bert n' Alf. I'm Alf and he's Bert and this is what we look like.

CRISPIN

I work for Donald. What has David Litvinoff told you about the film?

BERT
(snapping)
Nothin' as per usual. He's not here is he.

ALF

He said --

CRISPIN

-- OK, so it's called "Performance" and it's starring Mick, James Fox and Anita Pallenberg. The character – played by James – is a...
(looks up at ALF)
... how do you cats describe yourselves?

ALF

Cats?

BERT

Howd'ya mean?

CRISPIN

Gangsters? Criminals? Mobsters?

ALF FROWNS.

ALF

Us? Nah, we're just a couple o' Chaps. We're not villains.

BERT

We're self employed that's all.

ALF

That's right, we don't work for anyone.

BERT

Well we do, Alf. We work for *ourselves*. We're not idle. We're not spongers.

CRISPIN
(regarding the notebook)

OK, whatever ... so look, the lead character, Chas Devlin, he's hiding out from cats like you in a large house owned by Mick's character.

CRISPIN LOOKS ALF AND BERT UP AND DOWN. HE WALKS AROUND THEM.

CRISPIN

You both certainly look the part.

CRISPIN SQUEEZES HIS CHIN WITH FINGER AND THUMB AND NODS HIS HEAD. BERT AND ALF STAND STILL, BOTH A LITTLE SELF CONSCIOUS.

CRISPIN

Mmm. You look authentic ... this is the look Donald's after.

BERT

What "look"? I don't know nothing about being authentic. He never said anything.

ALF

Litvinoff tell ya we're not actors did he?

CRISPIN

It's not important. Donald doesn't want actors.

ALF
(confused)
Don't want actors? But we thought ...

BERT

We've not acted before. We're not even actors anyway.

ALF

Bert's right. We're not gonna lie to you.

BERT

Litvinoff said it were a picture so we thought ya wanted actors? Or *pretend* actors. You know, in the background. Make up the numbers or summink.

CRISPIN

It's fine. He wants blank canvasses.

BERT

Blank canvas? Howd'ya mean?

CRISPIN

He wants to paint pictures on you.

ALF AND BERT ARE PUZZLED. CRISPIN
GRABS A CHAIR AND PULLS IT TO THE
MIDDLE OF THE ROOM. HE SITS DOWN,
CROSSES HIS LEGS, OPENS HIS
NOTEBOOK AND PREPARES TO TAKE
NOTES. CRISPIN TAPS HIS TEETH WITH
THE PEN AND THEN POINTS AT ALF.

CRISPIN

Right. Just tell me a little about yourself. Go!

ALF

(pointing at himself)

Me?

CRISPIN

Let me hear you speak ... huh ... what's your name again?

ALF

Alf ... huh, short for Alfred. Everyone calls me Alf though.

CRISPIN

(jots the name down)

That's good ... go ahead, Alf. Talk to me, man.

ALF

(frowning)

Huh ... what about, like?

CRISPIN

Anything, everything. Just talk ... improvise.

ALF

(ALF glances at BERT for a
cue. BERT simply sighs.
After a beat)

All right. Huh ... name's Alf. Alfred Cutler ... mmm ...

CRISPIN

Go on, Alf. Don't stop.

ALF

Well, huh ... I ... I don't really know what t' say t' be honest.

CRISPIN

Anything. Say *anything*. I just want to get an idea of your rhythm, your pitch, your inflections.

ALF

My what?

CRISPIN

How you sound. We need authenticity. You need to sound right.

BERT
(defensive, pointing at ALF)

I've known him donkey's n' he's always sounded the same. He's always sounded *right*. I can vouch for that.

CRISPIN
(to BERT)

You're not understanding me.
(to ALF)

There's a certain rhythm that Donald's looking for. A kind of poetry.

BERT
(spitting it out)

Bleedin' poetry?

ALF

Litvinoff never said nothin' about no poetry.
(to BERT)

Did he say anything about poetry t' you?

BERT

We don't do poems, sunshine. Do we look like we do poems? We ain't Shakespeare.

CRISPIN

No, no, no. I mean ... listen ...
(sits back)
Just tell me a story. Talk to me about anything. Tell me a *funny* story.

ALF

A funny story? What about?

CRISPIN

Anything. You must have some funny stories, man like you.
Some tales. Make me laugh with a funny story.

ALF

(muttering)
Funny stories. Let me think ... I can't think to be honest. Can't think off
the top of me head ... mmm ... let's have a look ... can *you* think, Bert?

BERT

(to CRISPIN)
Listen, son. We're not a couple o' clowns. We're not a pair o' performin'
seals in a circus....now, listen, Litvinoff never mentioned cash. What sort
o' cash we lookin' at here?

CRISPIN

(a little affronted)
Cash? What do you mean?

BERT

Money. Lolly. How much we getting paid for this?
(beat)
Payment.

CRISPIN

Yeah, I know what bread is, man.

BERT

So...?

CRISPIN SNORTS, A LITTLE
INCREDULOUSLY.

CRISPIN

We haven't hired you yet. You haven't got the gig yet and talking bread's
so bourgeois anyway.

ALF

I think what Bert's sayin' is --

BERT

-- I know what I'm sayin', Alf. I'm talkin' readies.

CRISPIN

Renumeration will be discussed once we've finished all the auditions.

BERT

We ain't interested in no *renumeration* and Litvinoff said nothin' about
no auditions. How can *we* audition? We already told you we're not actors.
Why's Litvinoff not here?

CRISPIN

You'd have to ask *him*.

BERT

I *would* ask him if he were here! How can I ask him why he's not here
when he hasn't shown up!

CRISPIN
(sighing)
The only people we've signed up are Johnny Shannon and John Bindon.

ALF

Yeah, we know 'em. I worked with Johnny Shannon in the print.

CRISPIN

David should have told you more about it.

BERT

He never said a peep. Litvinoff's a bleedin' liability. He's a sneaky ratbag.
He's got his head so far up his own arse he can see his kidneys on a clear
day.

CRISPIN

He told us he'd told you. He said he'd filled you in on what was required.

BERT

He said nothin' of the bleedin' sort to us, did he, Alf?

ALF

I reckon I'd have remembered if he'd mentioned requirements n'
auditions and what have you.

BERT

Litvinoff says a lot o' things but you can't get any sense out of him.

ALF
(to CRISPIN)

Yeah, in all fairness I'll vouch for that. He does tend to talk a bit o'
gobbledegook.

BERT

He could send a glass eye to sleep ... he don't know the meanin' of the
word *bleedin' silence*. You take his cakehole away n' he's finished. You
might as well cut his legs off at the knee you take his gob away. He can
give you jaw-ache just lookin' at him.

CRISPIN
(impatient)
Look, it's not important. I just need to check you both out.
See if you fit. It's just about the rhythm. That's what Donald wants. Go
ahead … just talk.

ALF
You just want us to talk? Have a natter? N' I can talk about anything?

CRISPIN NODS HIS HEAD. ALF RUBS
AT HIS CHIN AND STARTS TO PACE. BERT
ALTERNATES A GLARE AT CRISPIN AND
A LOOK OF SYMPATHY TO BERT.

BERT
You all right, Alfred? You look a bit peeved.

ALF
Yeah, yeah, no, no … just havin' a think.

CRISPIN STARTS JOTTING. BERT
WATCHES ALF STRESSING OVER WHAT
TO SAY.

BERT
You sure you're good, Alf? You look a bit flummoxed. You look a bit
perturbed.

ALF
Yeah, yeah … mmm …

BERT
(quietly)
This is out of order.

CRISPIN

What was that?

BERT

Nothin'. I'm just sayin'.

ALF CLICKS HIS FINGERS, POINTS HIS
INDEX FINGER UPWARDS AND WAGS IT.

ALF

I've got it!

CRISPIN

Good, good, go ahead.

BERT

Wait a minute. What you got, Alf? What you remembered?

ALF EXCITEDLY CLOSES IN ON BERT.
THEY CONVERSE QUIETLY. CRISPIN
WATCHES THEM AND CONTINUES JOTTING.

ALF

You remember that time with Old Ginger and the sawn off?

BERT

Ginger? Yeah. He was the best Pavement Artist around God bless him.

ALF

Remember that time down Tooting when we hid a sawn off for him up
that grocers down in all them marrows? You remember.

BERT
(slowly nods his head in
recognition, a forced
chuckle)
Oh yeah, course I do, we shoved it in that big punnet o' Brussel sprouts.

ALF

Marrows. It weren't Brussels, Bert. It were marrows.

BERT

Same thing, veg' ... yeah, Old Bill were everywhere.

ALF

Swarming.

THEY ARE BOTH ON THE VERGE OF
BREAKING INTO LAUGHTER.

BERT

That Greengrocers face.

ALF

It were a picture. Pillock.

BERT

I know, I remember. It were a sight. *Soppy sod.*

ALF

Ginger scarpered. He was up that drainpipe like a rat. He was like Tarzan
he was! *Johnny Weismuller.*

BERT

'N that copper's mug. Flabbergasted!

ALF

Lost for words he was.

BERT

Mug. Speechless. He was talkin' gibberish.

ALF AND BERT LAUGH OUT LOUD.

ALF

What do you reckon?

BERT

Well ... it's a good story. It's funny.

ALF

Yeah, everyone pissed their pants.

BERT

I don't know about any pants bein' pissed, but yeah, it's funny. I'll give ya that. *He* probably won't understand it though. What does this berk know about the Old Bill n' Brussels n' Ginger n' his sawn off?

ALF

Alright, yeah, good point ... I know, I'll just tell him a joke.

BERT

Which joke?

ALF

There's that one about the two Irishmen walking down the street. They're walking down the street n' they see this dog licking its balls. Paddy turns to Mick and says "I wish I could do that?". Mick turns to Paddy and says, "Ugh! Why do you wanna lick a dog's balls you filthy bleeder?"
ALF laughs, BERT simply frowns ...

BERT

I don't get it. He obviously means he wishes he could lick his *own* plums *not* the dog's.

ALF

Yeah, yeah, but he's *Irish* ain't he?

BERT

It don't tickle *me*, Alf.

CRISPIN CUTS IN. HE PULLS OUT
A SHEET FROM THE NOTEBOOK AND
REGARDS IT.

CRISPIN

I don't suppose you guys are familiar with Borges?

BERT

Who?

CRISPIN

Borges.

BERT

Never heard of him. Who's he when he's at home?

CRISPIN

Jorge Luis Borges. A famous writer, philosopher. Argentinian.

BERT

No, we've never heard o' no writers have we, Alf?

ALF

Mmm ... I think I *have* heard of him now you mention it.

BERT
(suspicious, to ALF)

How've *you* heard of him? You've never said anythin' before.

ALF

I dunno. I just have. He's a writer or summink.

BERT

He just told you he's a writer. Yer getting mixed up wi' someone else.

CRISPIN

The film's inspired by Borges. Donald's a great admirer.

ALF

Litvinoff might o' said summink. I've heard the name. It rings a bell.

BERT

Well it's the first I'm hearing about him. Foreign is he?

CRISPIN STANDS AND PACES.

CRISPIN

Listen to this ...

CRISPIN

(reads from the sheet)

"Borges, I think, was always aware of this intense dualism. We have a dual nature. We are physical beings who live in the continuum of time, and we are also language users. Language enables us to take pieces out of our lived time, and to move them out of time in the form of what Borges called a "fiction": poems, essays, stories, they are all fictions."

CRISPIN LOOKS AT THEM TO CATCH
THEIR REACTION. ALF AND BERT
DON'T REACT.

CRISPIN

(reading)

"...A fiction is a construct of language, and we make fictions to make sense out of a reality which we fail to understand. Our fictions are attempts to bring the world into order for the time being, but unless we continue to believe in them, they dissolve like smoke."

(beat, to ALF and BERT)

Do you get that? Do you dig what he's saying?

ALF

Yeah. He's, huh ... he's talkin' about stories.

BERT

(to CRISPIN, pointing at his
notebook)

What's all that bumfluffery gotta do with this picture?

CRISPIN

Everything. It's got *everything* to do with the film. Donald's going to explore man's dualism. That's the theme.

ALF

So ... huh, this "dualism" lark's about being two faced, eh?

BERT

We've met some right two faced berks in our time. Met some right slippery sods haven't we, Alf? *We* could write a story about some o' the two-faced toads we've come across.

ALF

Yeah, villains aren't the most honest o' people.

CRISPIN

Dualism's not exactly about being two faced. It's more about ... huh,
(flounders)
... by the way, before I forget, do you guys have any hang ups about being naked?

ALF AND BERT GLANCE AT EACH OTHER.

BERT

How d'ya mean, *naked?*

ALF

Yeah, what's *naked* mean?

CRISPIN

It means no clothing. Naked. Naked on film...naked *in* the film.

BERT AND ALF TURN TO EACH OTHER.
BOTH SHOCKED.

ALF

You want us naked? In the picture? In the all together?

CRISPIN

There will be *some* scenes, some nudity, yeah.

BERT

(affronted)

You want us t' strip?!

ALF

Down to our birthday suits?

CRISPIN

Donald's been studying some of Francis Bacon's work. He's keen to film some tableaus. Tableaus of male nudity. There's a couple of scenes he's planning. They're going to look really beautiful.

BERT AND ALF ARE STILL LOOKING AT
EACH OTHER, NOT KNOWING HOW TO
REACT. BERT LOOKS AT CRISPIN.

ALF

What sort o' picture *is* this? Litvinoff never said nothing about bein' stark bollock naked.

BERT

Is this a foreign picture or summink?

ALF

We're not foreign, so --

CRISPIN

-- listen, you're --

BERT

-- is this some sort o' porno? A titty flick with sweaty arses everywhere? Is that what it is? Got us here under false pretences has he? Wait 'til I get my hands on that conniving little basket!

ALF
(putting his hands up in
surrender, shaking his head)
I'm not getting me kit off in no stag film. No way. I like a blue movie as
much as much as the next man but ... nah.

BERT
We'd be a bleedin' laughin' stock! Never live it down. My three piece
splashed all over Soho, every punter in town tuggin' off over my bare arse.
Our Hampton's on display for every man and his dog to toss off over! No
thank you very much!

ALF THINKS ABOUT IT AND SHUDDERS.
HE CLOSES IN ON CRISPIN, SHAKING
HIS HEAD.

ALF
Albert's right. I gotta agree with him, sunshine. I don't know what
Litvinoff told ya but he's bang out of order. We're not pornography actors!
Nobody's gonna pay good money t' see me n' Bert runnin' round flashing
our goolies, n' even if they did pay we still wouldn't do it.

BERT
Litvinoff's off his rocker if he thinks we'd be up for starrin' in a sleazy
porno!

CRISPIN LAUGHS AND SHAKES HIS HEAD.
ALF AND BERT ARE NOT AMUSED.

CRISPIN
No, no, no, no...it's not *pornographic*. It's integral to the story ... look, are
you familiar with the painter Francis Bacon's work?

ALF
(curious)

I've not seen his paintings but I've seen him in The Colony n' The French a few times. We're on noddin' terms. I know he's a poof but he seems all right. Always sloshed n' really loud but he's harmless. Why? Is he in this picture?

BERT

I know he paints pictures n' likes a drink, bit of a piss artist. He likes a bet, seen him in the bookies down the corner on Wardour Street. I don't know nothin' about gettin' me tackle out in no picture though!

CRISPIN

You're getting the wrong impression.

BERT SNORTS AND THROWS HIS HANDS
UP IN EXASPERATION.

BERT

"Wrong impression?" What *right* impression do you expect us to get? What exactly did that runt Litvinoff tell you about us, eh? Tell ya we were a couple o' nancy boys did he? Tell you we take it up the arse did he?

CRISPIN

Litvinoff said nothing of the sort. This isn't a pornographic picture we're making. It's a serious study of male identity, man.

BERT
(muttering to himself)

I'll have his guts for garters I will.

CRISPIN PULLS OUT SOME XEROXES OF
BACON'S PAINTINGS AND HANDS THEM
TO BERT AND ALF.

CRISPIN

Look, here, look at these. These are some of Bacon's paintings.

BERT AND ALF LOOK THROUGH THE
FRANCIS BACON XEROXES. BERT IS
CLEARLY NOT IMPRESSED AND HE TUTS
AND SCOWLS. ALF IS STUDYING THEM.

BERT

I could do these in me sleep n' I can't even draw.

CRISPIN

What do *you* see, Alf?

ALF
(flicking through the images)

Me? ... Mmm ... big fat shouty faces ... cages ... monsters ... ugly mugs ...
big fat arses ... slabs o' meat ... couple o' fellas wrestlin'... this is what ya
call that abstract modern art ain't it?

BERT
(handing his share of the
copies to ALF)

It's what ya call a load of old bollocks. This Bacon's takin' the piss. He's a
fanny merchant.

ALF

I'm not a big lover of art meself. I like a nice landscape o' race horses.
Couple o' nice lookin' nags on some grass in a paddock or a field.

CRISPIN

Do you understand what he's trying to say though?

ALF

I wouldn't have 'em hanging about in me dinin' room to be honest ...
they're a bit ...

CRISPIN

A bit what?

ALF

A bit violent lookin'... bit ... off – puttin'.

CRISPIN
(claps his hands together,
smiles and points at ALF)
Exactly! You've got it! You've got it, man!

ALF FROWNS AT CRISPIN AND BERT
SNORTS.

ALF
(unsure)
Have I? You sure?

CRISPIN

Sure, sure. There's a malevolence in Bacon's art. You get it.
You're perceptive.

BERT

People'll buy anything. He's having their drawers down.

CRISPIN

All art is subjective, Bert. *You* might find it worthless but to some people
it's beautiful ... it's all subjective.

BERT THINKS BETTER OF TRYING TO
REPLY. ALF IS STILL PERUSING THE
XEROXES.

ALF

Well ... if people wanna buy 'em good luck to him I say. If he can make a few bob that's all that matters ain't it.

ALF HANDS THE SHEETS BACK TO
CRISPIN. CRISPIN SLIPS THEM BACK
IN HIS NOTEBOOK.

BERT

They got more money than sense they have. One born every bleedin' minute. I wouldn't hang those things in me khazi. I wouldn't piss on 'em if they was on fire. Wouldn't wipe me arse with 'em.

ALF

Good luck to him I say. If berks are dozy enough t' pay for it ... well, more fool them.

CRISPIN
(to ALF)
But you did pick up on the integral malevolence though?

ALF

The what?

CRISPIN

The muted violence, Alf. The primal scream in the face of brutal and indifferent existence. Bacon's characters are all trapped in a futile existence. They are wallowing in prisons of their own making ...

CRISPIN PULLS OUT A NEWSPAPER
CLIPPING FROM THE NOTEBOOK.

CRISPIN

Listen ...

(he reads)

"For Bacon's is not fundamentally an art of exaggeration: it is the
exaggerations in ourselves which we dread to recognise. Bacon's art reveals
to us, often for the first time, and with the impact of prophecy, the true
nature of the world we live in ... and are the events which Bacon sets
before us more dreadful than those of which we read every day in the
newspapers?"

CRISPIN REGARDS ALF.

CRISPIN

Do you get that, Alf?

BERT

(to CRISPIN)

We're not here t' talk about art n' Bacon. We're supposed t' be here t' talk
about pictures, n' I'm not sayin' another dickie bird 'til you start talkin'
dosh.

CRISPIN

(slowly shakes his head,
regards BERT indifferently)

To be honest, I don't think you've got the right attitude to be in the film
anyway.

BERT OPENS HIS MOUTH TO RESPOND.
HE STARES AT CRISPIN BUT WORDS
DON'T FORM. ALF REALIZES BERT IS
SHOCKED AND STEPS IN TO DIFFUSE
THE SITUATION.

ALF
(to CRISPIN)
Nah, nah, he's not sayin' he *don't* wanna be in your --

CRISPIN
-- we don't want anyone involved who isn't one hundred percent
  committed to Donald's vision.

BERT
(pointing at CRISPIN)
You just wanna cop an eyeful o' me Old Man you do.

BERT CLOSES IN ON CRISPIN. CRISPIN
WAVES BERT AWAY. ALF CLOSES IN
BETWEEN BERT AND CRISPIN.

ALF
(to CRISPIN)
Listen, Cris, I --

CRISPIN
-- *Crispin.*

ALF
Listen, son. Here's a thought ... how naked would you want us?

CRISPIN
How naked?

ALF
Yeah.

BERT
Don't be a berk, Alf. He wants us in our bleedin' birthday suits!

CRISPIN

I don't really -- what don't you understand about being naked, Alf?

ALF

Yeah, I know, I know, but just how much *nakedness* would ya want off us? What I mean is, huh ... let me put it another way ... would ya want *full* naked or could we keep our scivvies on?

CRISPIN

The point of being naked is that you don't have *any* clothes on. If you've got worries over nudity I'll just have to --

ALF

-- whoa, hold yer horses, Cris. Don't be jumping to conclusions. We're always lookin' to make a few bob. You got the wrong end o' the stick. Nobody's sayin' anythin' about *not* gettin' naked.

BERT PUTS HIS HAND ON ALF'S
SHOULDER AND TURNS HIM AROUND.

BERT

Oi! *You* might not be sayin' anythin' about not gettin' naked but I am! *I'm* sayin' summink! It's not on! Not on yer bleedin' Nelly!

CRISPIN

I really think *you're* good for the part, Alf. I think you could bring something ... this could turn out to be a real opportunity for you.

ALF

How'd ya mean?

CRISPIN NARROWS HIS GAZE ON ALF
AND CIRCLES HIM, GETTING HIS
MEASURE. BERT FOLDS HIS ARMS AND
LEANS BACK AGAINST A TABLE EDGE.

CRISPIN

Acting. You could get noticed, man. Yeah, definitely.

BERT

Oh he'd *get noticed* with his spotty old arse flapping about all right!

ALF

(waves his hand at CRISPIN:

get away)

Don't be daft, son. I'm not an actor n' I'm definitely not a nude actor. *Get away.*

CRISPIN

No, I'm serious … yeah, yeah … you've got … presence.

ALF

Presence? Me? Pull the other one. I'm just little old Alf. I jus' do a bit o' duckin' n' divin'. I ain't got any ideas above me station, Cris.

CRISPIN

Crispin, and no, no, I mean it. You could easily get noticed.

BERT

He'll get noticed all right. He'll get noticed by the fuckin' Vice Squad. They'll have him in front of a beak before he can pull his socks up.

CRISPIN

There's a call for men like you nowadays.

ALF

Is there? Men like me, eh.

ALF IS CLEARLY FEELING A LITTLE
FLATTERED NOW.

ALF

Even if I'm not a proper actor? Even if I've never done any?

CRISPIN

Why not? You could carve out a career for yourself. You could become famous.

ALF

Get away. You hear him, Bert?

BERT

Famous? Kiss o' death to chaps like us! Last thing you wanna be is famous when yer tryin' to earn a few bob, Alf.

ALF
(to CRISPIN)

Give over. Yer havin' yerself on.
(to BERT)

He reckons I could get away with pretending t' be an actor.

BERT

He's butterin' you up. Listen t' yerself. He's fannyin' you.

ALF

Yer windin' me up you are, Cris.

CRISPIN

Crispin, and why would I do that?

BERT

Let's just fuck off, Alf.

CRISPIN

There are plenty of young directors wanting to work with people like you ... you've got authenticity, man.

ALF THINKS ABOUT IT. HE SEES BERT
SHAKING HIS HEAD AND THEN REGARDS
CRISPIN.

BERT

Load of old rhubarb.

ALF

I dunno ... you really think so, eh, Cris?

CRISPIN

Pictures are changing. The rules are being torn up. That's where Donald Cammell's coming from. He's of the avant garde. The 1970's are just around the corner. It's a new age.

ALF

Mmm ... n' you really think I could make a few bob from acting?

CRISPIN

Good actors can make a fortune.

ALF

Yeah, I've read about 'em making a packet.

BERT
(to CRISPIN)

He's not an actor! How many times do we have t' tell ya!

ALF

I've never pretended t' be an actor. You ask anyone n' they'll tell you, "Alf's never pretended to be an actor". They'll say, "Alf? Alf an actor? Leave it out! Pull the other one! He's never done any actin' in his life. He's proud to say he's never stepped foot in a theatre. Good old Alf wouldn't been seen dead in a theatre."

CRISPIN

We all take on roles, Alf. That's life. That's what it means to be human, man. All the world's a stage, you know.

BERT
(snapping at CRISPIN,
gesturing "yapping")

You're giving it all that you are! But you should ask about. Ask about and find out who I am. I don't put up with bein' messed about like a pillock! Ask that berk Litvinoff if I like bein' messed about like a pillock. Ask that little Yid if I put up with liberty takers.
(to ALF)
Let's sling our hook. Let's fuck off.

ALF
(pacing, calculating)

I remember Bindon sayin' ya can make some good coin in the pictures. He said it's not just yer film stars either.

CRISPIN

This could be an opportunity for you, Alf. Get to meet some interesting people. Who knows what could happen once opportunity knocks.

BERT
(spitting it out in distaste)

Hughie Green! Opportunity Knocks? Bollocks!

ALF TURNS TO BERT.

ALF

He's got a point though ain't he, Bert?

BERT

A point? No! He's got a bleedin' cheek is what he's got. He's lucky I ain't
lost me rag with him ... he's lucky I don't chin toffee nosed little twerps
like him.

ALF
(diplomatic)
Come on, Albert. Nobody's gettin' chinned in here.

CRISPIN

Nobody's keeping *you* here, Bert.

BERT NARROWS HIS GAZE ON CRISPIN.

BERT

What's that supposed t' mean?

CRISPIN

Alf can see something. He gets it. You obviously don't ... that's cool, man.
I understand.

BERT

You know nothin' about me, son! Ask around! Ask anyone in London.
You know nothing about me, china, but I know all about your sort.

CRISPIN

My "sort"?

BERT

Fuckin' free love n' psychopathic drugs!

CRISPIN GIGGLES. BERT GLARES AT
HIM.

BERT

Who do you think you're chortling at? Don't you chortle at me, mush!
Tell him what happened to the last twerp that chortled at me, Alf.

ALF

Leave it out, Bert. We're just talking. Nobody's chortling.

BERT

He giggled. I heard him. I'm not deaf!

ALF

Nobody's sayin' yer deaf, Bert.

BERT

There's nothing wrong with *my* lugs. I heard every word of it.
He chortled.

CRISPIN

Look, can we just --

BERT

-- I don't even let my family laugh at me, do I Alf?
(pointing at CRISPIN)
Ask my bleedin' Brother in Law if I let my family laugh at *me*. Go on, go
ask him. See'f he thinks laughing's funny.

CRISPIN

Oh this is ridiculous!

BERT

Ridiculous, eh? *You* might think it's ridiculous but *I* take people laughing
at me seriously. I'm not Tony Hancock. I'm not the bleedin' Goon Show!
Do I look like Hancock's Half Hour to you or summink?

CRISPIN

Look, just listen, this is getting us nowhere. You're not right for a part in Performance. I've seen enough thanks.

BERT

What? What did you say? I heard what you said. Say that again.

CRISPIN

I said I've --

BERT

-- seen enough? *Seen enough?* You ain't seen nuffink, chum! I can show you things you wish you'd never seen. I can show you things that'll give you nightmares.

CRISPIN

Your attitude. It's all wrong. Alf – on the other hand – well --

BERT
(to Crispin)
-- you givin' me the "fuck off", china?
(to ALF)
Is he givin' me the elbow, Alf?

CRISPIN

You're just not right, that's all.

BERT

"Just not right?!" I don't even wanna be in yer stinkin' picture, but I'm not being given me marching orders by a queer little twerp like you.
(to ALF)
You hear that, Alf! He said I'm not right! He reckons I'm *wrong*!
Somebody should tell this ratbag what I'm capable of.
(to CRISPIN)
You got some bleedin' nerve tellin' me I'm wrong, son.

ALF

He don't mean yer *wrong*, Bert. He jus' means yer not right for this picture that's all.

BERT

I know what he means. He's showin' me the bleedin' door.
(to CRISPIN)
Givin' me my marching orders, eh? Handin' me, me P45, eh?

CRISPIN

I don't understand why you're getting so upset, Bert.

BERT

(snorts)
Upset! Who said I'm gettin' upset! I never get upset! I'll fuckin' show you "upset" you cunt!

BERT MAKES TO MOVE IN ON CRISPIN.
ALF CUTS HIM OFF. THEY ARE FACE
TO FACE. FOR A MOMENT IT LOOKS
LIKE THEY MIGHT GET TO BLOWS. ALF
PUTS HIS HAND ON BERT'S SHOULDER.

ALF

Nobody's gettin' chinned in here. He's a civvy.

BERT SIMMERS AND HEADS OVER TO THE DOOR.

BERT

Come on, Alf. Let's get on our toes.

ALF

I dunno, Bert ... Cris might be right ... it could be a good opportunity this. *This* could open up doors ...
(tries to make light)
It could be Opportunity Knocks With Hughie Green this. The old clapometer, eh?

BERT

Clapometer? Clap*trap* more like! Load o' bleedin' poncey nonsense!

ALF

But --

BERT

-- how many times do I have to tell you yer not an actor! You can't act for toffee! You couldn't act yer way out of a wet paper bag if yer life depended on it.

CRISPIN

Alf can stay if he likes, Bert.

BERT
(to ALF)
What's he say? I'm not listenin' to him anymore.

CRISPIN
(loud)
I said there's nothing keeping you here.

BERT
(to ALF)
Tell that twerp I heard him ... tell him I'm not deaf. I don't need me lugholes washin' out. I got perfect hearin' I have. 20/20 vision.

CRISPIN
(to BERT)
Why you being down on Alf, man? Alf digs all this.

BERT
(opening the door)
Let's sling our hook ... I've heard enough.
(stopping dead, pointing at
CRISPIN)
And *you*!...you, sunshine!

BERT STOPS HIMSELF FROM CONTINUING.
HE OPENS THE DOOR.

BERT
You comin' or what, Alf?

ALF PAUSES. HE LOOKS AT CRISPIN
AND THEN SHUFFLES ABOUT.

CRISPIN
I think Alf's staying. It looks like Alf's staying to me.

ALF LOOKS DOWN COYLY.

BERT
(beat)
That right is it, Alf?
(beat)
You stayin', eh? Abandoning the stinkin' ship, eh?

ALF SIGHS AND SHRUGS.

BERT
Well? ... you stayin' or what? ... yer either comin' or stayin'. You can't do
both, Alf.

ALF

Huh ... yeah ...

BERT

Good. Come on then.

ALF
(coy)
... I'm gonna give it a go, Bert. You get yerself over Brick Lane n' we'll have a drink later on, eh.

BERT GLARES AT ALF AND SHAKES HIS
HEAD.

BERT

Now *you're* givin' me the "fuck off" as well, eh?

ALF

Nobody's bein' fucked off, Bert ... it's just ... well, it's ... it's an opportunity. It's only a bit of actin'. Nobody's gonna get hurt.

BERT AND ALF STARE AT EACH OTHER.

BERT

I don't believe *you*, Alf. You surprise me ... you really surprise me you do ... I'm ... well, I'm surprised.

ALF

What? 'Cos I wanna earn a few honest nicker? What's surprising about that?

BERT
(shaking his head)
There's nothing *honest* about gettin' yer goolies out in a picture, Alf. Yer one step away from bein' a brass.

ALF

Don't talk bleedin' daft! I'm not selling me body for sex.

BERT

You might as well be. It's degrading.

ALF

Poppycock! Look, listen to me Bert, don't come the pillock. I'm a big boy n' I ain't doing nothing wrong. We'll have a good drink later on. I'll meet you in The Ship.

BERT AND ALF ARE STARING AT EACH OTHER. THEY HOLD THE STARE UNTIL ALF LOOKS AWAY. BERT GLARES AT CRISPIN AND THEN LEAVES, SLAMMING THE DOOR BEHIND HIM.

ALF

He's a bit airyated today, you caught him on a bad day that's all.

CRISPIN

He doesn't concern me.

CRISPIN SMILES AT ALF AND STEPS BACK, LOOKING HIM UP AND DOWN.

CRISPIN

So ... the picture.

ALF

Yeah, the picture.

CRISPIN

What do you think then?

                    ALF
About the picture?

                  CRISPIN
Yeah, man. I can tell you get it. You've got an angle on it.

                    ALF
Look, I'll be honest, I'm a grafter. If there's work t' be done I don't mind
gettin' me hands dirty.

                  CRISPIN
I think you'll bring something to it.

                    ALF
                 (frowning)
Bring summink?

                  CRISPIN
Yeah definitely. I think I'll probably recommend you to Donald.

              ALF IS FLATTERED.

                    ALF
Yeah? You'd do that, eh?

                  CRISPIN
Yeah. I'll definitely consider it.

                    ALF
               (snorts happily)
That's a turn up f' the books, eh.

                  CRISPIN
I'll probably recommend you then it's up to Donald.

ALF

Yeah, yeah, course ... still ... if someone had told me I was pretendin' to be an actor before I got here I'd o' thought they were pullin' me leg.

CRISPIN

Donald will have to see you as well.

ALF

He'll want a little dickie bird, eh?

CRISPIN

You'll like Donald if you get to meet him. He's a real artist.

ALF

He'll want to see me *here* will he?

CRISPIN

If I recommend you he might.

ALF

The only day I can't do is a Wednesday afternoon. I drive me Old Aunt Dotty down St. Thomas' with her veins n' we stop off at *Pie Herbert's* for some eels.

CRISPIN

He'll probably want to probe you.

ALF

(frowning, beat)

How'd ya mean *probe* me?

CRISPIN

Get into your head space. Get a hook on you, man.

ALF

(slowly nods his head)

Right, right you are. Talk to me? I get it.

CRISPIN

You might get to meet Mick as well. *Mick Jagger.*

ALF

I seen him in a few drinkin' holes as it happens. We're on noddin' terms. Always got a blindin' bit o' crumpet on his arm.

CRISPIN

This film wouldn't be getting made if it weren't for Mick's involvement. There's only Mick could play Turner. The part's been written for him.

ALF

He likes a bit of actin' then, eh? He'll be lookin' to make a few bob when he can't do the old Hit Parade thing anymore.

CRISPIN

Yeah, maybe ... so ... ready when you are then, Alf.

ALF

Eh?

CRISPIN

Ready when *you* are.

ALF

For what?

CRISPIN

I told you. Donald will want you naked in a couple of scenes. I need to be able to tell him you don't have any problems with it.

ALF

(gulps, beat)

Now? In here?

CRISPIN

Sure.

ALF PAUSES AND THINKS ABOUT IT.

CRISPIN

I can't even think about possibly recommending you to Donald if you can't perform something as simple as getting naked, man.

ALF

So ... so if I don't peel off there's no chance o' me getting a go on this picture then?

CRISPIN

I'm not pressuring you ... if you don't think you can do it.

ALF

Do you have to watch?

CRISPIN

Obviously. How would I know if you were naked?

ALF

You could close yer eyes n' I could tell ya.

CRISPIN

No, no, like I said, it's important that you're comfortable being nude.

ALF

There's no funny business in all this, eh?

CRISPIN

What do you mean?

ALF

I mean, it's kosher, yeah? All above board?

CRISPIN

There's nothing *funny* about it, Alf. It's *strictly* business. The business of art. Do you think Mick Jagger would be involved if there was anything unsavory involved?

ALF

Mmm ... yeah ... I suppose yer right.

CRISPIN WATCHES ALF PACE. ALF TAKES
A DEEP BREATH AND GRABS A CHAIR. HE
STARTS TO UNDRESS.

ALF

All right ... in for a penny.

ALF METICULOUSLY FOLDS HIS JACKET,
SHIRT AND TROUSERS ON THE CHAIR
UNTIL HE IS WEARING ONLY A
PRISTINE WHITE VEST, Y-FRONTS AND
BLACK SOCKS WITH SOCK GARTERS. HE
TURNS TO CRISPIN.

ALF

Is this all right for now?

CRISPIN

But you're not naked, Alf.

ALF

Huh, yeah yeah yeah, but ... well, you get the picture, eh?

CRISPIN
(mock sympathetic)
If you can't get naked in front of *me*, how you going to get naked in front of a camera crew and all the other actors?

ALF THINKS ABOUT IT AND STARTS TO
PSYCHE HIMSELF UP.

ALF
What if our Florence walks in?

CRISPIN
She won't. I told her not to disturb us.

ALF PAUSES THEN TAKES OFF HIS
VEST. HE FOLDS IT AND PUTS IT ON
THE PILE OF HIS OTHER CLOTHES ON
THE CHAIR. HE TURNS TO CRISPIN.

ALF
(resigned)
Me scivvies as well, eh?

CRISPIN
Mmm.

ALF
I can leave me socks on though, eh?

CRISPIN NODS HIS HEAD. ALF SLOWLY
STARTS TO PEEL HIS Y-FRONTS DOWN.
ON THIS BERT STOMPS THROUGH THE
DOOR. ALF QUICKLY STOPS PEELING HIS
Y-FRONTS OFF AND PULLS THEM UP.

BERT

I forgot me Mirror!

ON SEEING ALF PULLING HIS Y-
FRONTS UP, BERT STOPS DEAD IN HIS
TRACKS AND GLARES AT ALF. HE IS
SPEECHLESS. ALF LOOKS DOWN.
BERT SLOWLY PICKS UP HIS
NEWSPAPER AND TUTS.

BERT
(shaking his head, spitting
it out)

I hope yer proud of yerself, Alf! This is a bleedin' embarrassment. It's an
outrage! Grown middle aged man o' your age ... just look at ya! Yer a
bleedin' eyesore.

CRISPIN
(to BERT)

Alf can do whatever he wants.

BERT

I ain't tellin' him he can't you cunt! I'm tellin' him for his own good. He's
well respected. He's well liked. Everyone's got a good word for Alf. He's
stand-up he is.

ALF
(quietly)

I'm all right, Bert.

BERT

He's a pillar o' the community. Nobody's got a bad word for him. He
sets a good example he does, he's a saint ... I got a good mind t' tell The
Chaps what yer up to, Alf.

ALF

What did you say?

BERT

You heard me, Alf.

ALF STARES AT BERT.

ALF

Eh? No I didn't. What's that supposed to mean, "tell The Chaps..."?

BERT

(pleading)

This ain't *you*, Alf. Yer above flashin' yer plums at some hippy ponce in a rotten bleedin' office. It's a slippery slope.

ALF

What you on about?

BERT

You start lobbin' yer Hampton out in here one minute n' the next minute yer starrin' in blue movies with schvarzers n' rancid old whores. Every lowlife cunt on the manor wankin' off over ya.

ALF POINTS AT BERT.

ALF

(stern)

This is between us, Bert. It goes no further you hear?

BERT

The Chaps'd agree with me. It's below you. Yer above this.

ALF STORMS OVER TO BERT. HE GETS
IN HIS FACE.

ALF

This has got nothing t' do wi' The Chaps. It's none o' their bleedin' business.

BERT

I'm just sayin' that's all. If The Chaps --

ALF

-- no yer not! Yer not *"just sayin'"*. Yer threatenin'. You best keep yer beak out you hear? You best shut yer trap n' keep yer neb out! The Chaps don't need to know nothin'.

BERT

But --

ALF

-- but button it! But nish! Your cakehole stays shut!

BERT

They're gonna find out when they're sat in some peep show down Berwick Street tossing off over ya. What they gonna think about *me* not warning 'em, eh?

ALF

It's not a bluey. It's arty. It's Francis bleedin' Bacon!

BERT

I don't care what it is. It's not right ... I can't guarantee I'll keep schtum.

ALF

Oh, is that right is it?

BERT

That's right.

ALF CLOSES IN FURTHER AND LEADS
BERT INTO A CORNER. HE TALKS
QUIETLY TO BERT.

ALF

I weren't gonna say nothin'. We all make mistakes.

BERT

What you --

ALF

-- you heard me. I heard *you*. I heard you yappin' to our Florence. I was earwiggin'. I heard everythin'. Not a pretty sight. Me ears were burnin'.

BERT GULPS AND HIS POSTURE
SLUMPS. ALF STARTS TO WHISPER IN
BERT'S EAR.

ALF

I heard what you was sayin' when I came back from The Bookies. I overheard the talk. I heard you givin' it all that about spunkin' up n' Rubber Johnny's.

BERT

(panicked)

Hold on a minute. I can explain.

ALF

I were gonna keep schtum, mum's the word. She was gonna lose her cherry one day. There's no point havin' aggro over a bit o' slap n' tickle, but ... well ... our Kenny won't see it like that will he? Nah, his *daughter*, his first born bleedin' daughter. Think about it. He gave birth to her. He brought her into this world.
She's his little Princess, she's his flesh n' blood, she's the twinkle in his eye, she's his sugar n' spice n' all things bleedin' nice n' you ... *you* deflowered little Florence you did.

BERT BOWS HIS HEAD.

BERT

I was out of order, I didn't know she was Kenny's Daughter. I thought she was Teddy's ... I .. I ... I had it off with her by accident, Alf.

ALF

That might well the case but --

BERT

-- it is, it is. On me Mother's eyes.

ALF

I weren't there so I'm not gonna judge, but Our Kenneth'll judge ya. *He* won't believe you had it off by accident.

BERT

Two wrongs ain't right though, Alf. There's no need for you to star in a dirty picture. I don't wanna see you in a porno. Nobody does!

ALF

Look, listen to me ... you just think on what our Kenny would do before you go tellin' The Chaps about *me* ... nobody wants another war, but *he's* not bothered. Kenny's done his stretch n' his blood's up. One word from me n' he'd rip you from arsehole to earhole. He'd go to war on his todd. He'd take you apart at the bleedin' seams n' leave you where he found ya. He'd kick ten shades o' shit out of ya, he'd rip your spleen out n' make mincemeat. He'd marmalize ya at the drop of an hat.

BERT

Listen, Alf, I --

ALF

-- The Chap's ain't gonna hear nothin' about this. Nobody is ... you got that?

BERT NODS HIS HEAD.

ALF

You hear me, Albert? If The Chaps did hear about it I'd know who they'd heard it from wouldn't I?

BERT NODS HIS HEAD AGAIN. ALF
BACKS OFF A LITTLE.

BERT
(beat, cowed)
Yer right, Alf. It were an accident that got out of hand that's all. She ... well, she egged me on n' --

ALF PUTS HIS HAND UP INDICATING
BERT TO "STOP".

ALF

-- everyone knows what these young bints are like nowadays. They can't wait t' get their leg over, they think they're older than they really are, but nobody wants to go to war over a bit of *hows yer father*.

BERT
(apologetic)
I wouldn't o' really told The Chaps, Alf.

ALF PAUSES AND SMILES. HE SOFTENS
AND PATS BERT ON THE SHOULDER.

ALF

I know, I know. Things get said that nobody means. We're all guilty of it. Bang to rights. *Guilty yer honour*. Loose lips sink ships. Verbal diarrhea. We all get it sometimes.

BERT

Yer right, Alf, I'm sorry ... nobody's perfect.

ALF

That's right. It's common sense.

BERT NODS HIS HEAD AT ALF. ALF
PINCHES BERT'S CHEEK.

BERT

Now, you get yerself over Brick Lane n' give that rotten old Yid a good
clump, eh...
give him one for me as well, give him a kick up the arse n' tell him I was
askin' after him, eh... we'll have a good drink later.

ALF

Yeah.

BERT

Bygones be bygones. No use crying over spilt milk.

BERT

No. You're right.

BERT SMILES AT ALF AND LEAVES.
ALF GOES OVER TO CRISPIN, RUBS
HIS HANDS TOGETHER AND SMILES.

ALF

Albert's salt o' the earth. He's just a bit old fashioned.

CRISPIN

He's not right for the part.

ALF

I've always been open minded about making a few bob. I mean, me n' the
missus are off to that Tory-Mo-Lean-Os for a jolly. It's in Spain allegedly.
We're flying there.

CRISPIN

Can we --

ALF

-- not cheap mind, hundred nicker. It'll be the first time we've tried flying. We'll be on one o' them aeroplanes though.

CRISPIN

Cool, huh, do you want to ...

ALF LOOKS DOWN AT HIS Y-FRONTS.

ALF

Oh, yeah, right you are.

FLORENCE ENTERS HOLDING A BUNCH OF LETTERS AND ALF PUTS HIS HANDS ACROSS HIS GROIN. FLORENCE SHAKES HER HEAD WHEN SHE SEES ALF.

FLORENCE

What're you ...

ALF

Oh, uh, I'm doin' an audition ain't I?

FLORENCE IS DUBIOUS

FLORENCE

Why you got yer clothes off, Uncle?

CRISPIN

What is it you want?

FLORENCE

I just, I'm ... I'm off up the Post Office. There anything you need posting?

CRISPIN

No.

ALF TAKES FLORENCE TO THE SIDE.

ALF
(to CRISPIN)
Give us a minute, Cris.
(quietly)
Listen Florence, I know this looks a bit queer, but --

FLORENCE
-- I don't like the look o' this, Uncle.

ALF
No, me neither, but it's not whatcha think. It's art innit.

FLORENCE
Is it?

ALF
It's whatchamacallit.

FLORENCE
What?

ALF
Artistic. All the actors are doing it nowadays.

FLORENCE
You're not an actor though.

ALF
No, not a proper one. Not yet, but, look, listen to me, Florence. You don't have to tell anyone about this, right?

FLORENCE

Tell who?

ALF

Anyone. People might get the wrong idea you go yapping about it. It's only an audition. I'd only take me clothes for an audition or a bath or summink.

FLORENCE

I don't like the look of it, Uncle.

ALF

I don't petal, nobody does but it's art, someone's gotta do it.

FLORENCE SIGHS AND SHAKES HER HEAD.

ALF

You gonna do as yer Uncle Alf says, treacle? Just keep schtum, eh?

FLORENCE

I dunno ... it's not right.

ALF
(sighing, snappier)
Yeah, well there's a lot o' things *not right* young lady. Blackmail's not right either is it?

FLORENCE

What'dya mean?

ALF

What do I mean? *You* know what I mean: having poor Bert's trousers down like that. I was earwiggin'. Our Kenneth won't be happy. We don't do blackmail in our family. We're decent people we are. He don't wanna be coming out The Scrubs hearing about his little girl blackmailing people does he? He won't be a happy chappy, I'd put good money on it.

FLORENCE

It's not like that.

ALF

What's it like then? I heard every word young lady. You extorted him …
now, you keep your trap shut about this bit of art n' I'll forget all about
what you did to poor Bert, all right?

FLORENCE THINKS ABOUT IT.

FLORENCE

Do it then.

ALF

Eh?

FLORENCE

Tell me Dad.

ALF

Hold on, wait a minute. I don't wanna get you in trouble, Flor --

FLORENCE
(defiant)
-- no, go on. Tell him you heard me n' Bert. Tell him everything.

ALF

Look, what I'm sayin --

FLORENCE

-- I don't think he'll happy about *you* knowing I went with Bert n' didn't
do nothing about it.

ALF

(slowly panicking)

You wouldn't dare tell your Old Man you've been up to no good. You're the apple of his eye. He'd take your head off he would. It'd put him in an early grave thinkin' you'd had a bit o' slap n' tickle with Bert.

FLORENCE

No, I mean it. Tell him, we can *both* tell him what happened. I'll tell him I came in here and saw Crispin bumming you!

ALF IS FLABBERGASTED.

ALF

Wash your mouth out with carbolic! Me? A shirtlifter? That's disgusting that is!

FLORENCE

And I'll tell him you knew about me and Bert havin' it off and you didn't do nish.

ALF

Jesus, Florence! What's got into you?

FLORENCE

I mean it, Uncle. I'll tell him you're a ponce if I have to.

ALF

You're not thinking straight, girl. You're discombobulated you are. A ponce indeed! *Me?* I've never been so insulted. You need to wash that mouth of yours out with soap. Your Dad would turn in his grave if he was dead.

FLORENCE

Well he ain't dead and I'm telling him! He won't be happy, Uncle. He'd do anything for me he would.

ALF
(really panicking now)
Florence, Florence, there's no need for anything like this. It's all a
misunderstanding. We're getting our knickers in a twist over summink
n' nothin', sweetheart. I won't say a dickie bird, I was talkin' rubbish, I
wasn't thinking straight. I'd never dob you in it, precious. I love you like a
niece. We don't need all this hurly burly my time o' life.

FLORENCE
(pretending to be on the
verge of tears)
Well you've got me goat. I'm upset now. I don't like being upset. I'm a lot
happier when I'm not upset.

ALF
I'm sorry, darling. I don't know what I was saying, it's me blood pressure.
The Quack's got me on these tablets and ... listen, look, listen to me petal.
Let's just forget all this happened, eh? I swear I won't say a word ... none
o' this ever happened, all right? I didn't hear nothing and you didn't see
nothing and we'll just forget it never happened in the first place, eh?

FLORENCE DABS AT HER EYES AND
SNIFFLES A LITTLE. SHE NODS HER
HEAD.

ALF
There's a good girl.

FLORENCE
Fifty quid.

ALF
(shocked)
Eh?

FLORENCE

You heard me.

ALF

No I didn't. You said summink about fifty quid.

FLORENCE

I *want* fifty quid.

ALF

What? What you want fifty quid for?

FLORENCE

For me. For me keeping schtum.

ALF

You've gotta be kidding! You're having a giraffe!

FLORENCE

I'm not kidding. I'm not mucking about.

ALF
(chuckling)

Yer winding me up you are.

FLORENCE

I ain't winding *anyone* up. I want fifty quid.

ALF
(snorting, half laughing)

This is cobblers! You're yankin' me chain you are. You can't do this to your little old Uncle Alf.

FLORENCE

I can and I will.

ALF

It's blackmail! Yer at it again! What the bleedin' hell's got into you? You're blackmail barmy you are!

FLORENCE

Yeah, well ...

ALF

I'm not helping you break the law young lady. I'm not aiding n' abetting extortion. I refuse to be blackmailed by my own flesh n' blood.

FLORENCE

All right, I'll tell him then.

ALF

But Florence, I -- look, if you need money I'll give it you, I'd give you me kidneys if ya wanted 'em, but I'm yer Uncle. I'm yer little Uncle Alf, you can't blackmail *me*. It's out of order, it's not right. You know it's wrong, yer a clever girl, you work in an office n' go to university 'n you make a blinding cuppa, you got a career. You can't be a blackmailer as well, Florence, it's illegal and it's wrong.

FLORENCE

Well it's fifty quid or I tell Dad *everything*.

ALF

You're really hurting me feelings, Florence. What about my bleedin' blood pressure!

FLORENCE

Yeah? Well you should o' thought about blood pressure before you let Crispin bum ya!

ALF

Where you gettin' all this bummin' rhubarb from?

FLORENCE

It's sick. Just the thought of it turns me stomach. My Dad knows I wouldn't make something up like that if it weren't true.

ALF

But it fuckin' well ain't true! Pardon my French.

FLORENCE

Yeah, but Dad don't know that, does he? He believes everything I say. He don't believe I'm a liar.

ALF OPENS HIS MOUTH TO SPEAK BUT
STOPS HIMSELF. HE PAUSES THEN ...

ALF

But Florence --

FLORENCE

-- cough up or I tell my Dad.

ALF

But, Flor --

FLORENCE

-- come on. I need to go The Post Office.

ALF

I've never been so ... do you know how hurt I am? I used to bounce you up n' down on my knee and now you're ... this is unbelievable. I don't believe it.

FLORENCE

Hurry up. I ain't got all day. I got things to do.

ALF

This is ...
                    (beat)
I'm ... I'm not holding at the minute. Can I give you it later?

FLORENCE
(suddenly upbeat)
Yeah, alright ... ta'ra, Uncle.

FLORENCE QUICKLY LEAVES. ALF
EXHALES LOUDLY AND RUBS AT HIS
TEMPLES.

ALF
(muttering, under his breath)
Schemin', conniving little ...

CRISPIN

Are you ready now?

ALF

Eh?

CRISPIN

Are you ready?

ALF

Oh, uh ...

CRISPIN

Are you all right?

ALF

Eh?

CRISPIN

Are you OK, Alf?

ALF

(quietly)

You think you know people.

CRISPIN

What's that?

ALF

Nothing. I'm just sayin', people can really surprise you.

CRISPIN

Well, yeah, for sure.

ALF

You think you know people, eh?

CRISPIN

Mmm. Life can be very surprising.

ALF

That's right. You can say that again. You never know what's round the bleedin'
corner. You're spot on, you've hit the nail right on the head, Cris.

CRISPIN

Crispin. I suppose life would be dull if there weren't any surprises.

ALF

True, true. I ain't got nothing against surprises, it's just ... I just don't like
they way they pop out at you.

CRISPIN

They wouldn't *be* surprises if they didn't *pop out* at you, Alf.

ALF

I know, but it'd wouldn't be so much of a shock if surprises gave you a bit of a warning beforehand. And listen, Cris, talking about surprises -- and don't take this the wrong way n' I'm not saying they would, but if anyone ever ...

CRISPIN

What?

ALF

If anyone ever asks if you've ...

CRISPIN

Go on.

ALF

If anyone ever asks if you've made love to me up my bum you just tell 'em --

CRISPIN

-- woah! Excuse me! Where did that come from? Why would anyone --

ALF

-- no, no, I'm not saying they *will* -- they won't. I'm just sayin' *if* they did.

CRISPIN
(frowning)
If anyone asks if I've "*made love to you*" up your ...?

ALF

They won't, just, you know, in case.

CRISPIN

I'm not homosexual, Alf, and even if I were ... well, I mean, no offense.

CRISPIN LOOKS ALF UP AND DOWN AND
SNORTS, INDICATIVE OF HIM NOT
BEING INTERESTED.

ALF

Yeah, no, yeah. I'm not fishing for compliments. I'm not suggesting
you fancy me. I'm probably too old for you and I don't think you're a
shirtlifter anyway, but just deny it if they ask -- which they won't. So, you
know ...

CRISPIN

I think I can manage that.

ALF

Good. It'll never happen anyway, but it's always best to be prepared, eh.

CRISPIN

How do you *prepare* for someone asking you a question like that?

ALF

Well you don't have to do you, cos it'll never happen. I'm being ... *there's a
bleedin' word for it*, mmm ...

CRISPIN

Hypothetical?

ALF

Nah, summink else. What's *that* word mean?

CRISPIN

Supposing. Supposing something *might* happen.

ALF

Yeah, nah you see there's not a bleedin' cat in hell's chance it'll happen.
No there's no supposing about it. It won't.

CRISPIN

You seem a bit worried about this, Alf.

ALF

Worried? Nah, nah, you've just gotta be careful nowadays. You never
know what people are gonna ask you.

CRISPIN

This is because you're undressing for me isn't it? You're worried someone
might say something.

ALF

Well it does look a bit ginger don't it, Cris?

CRISPIN

"Ginger"?

ALF

Ginger beer ... queer.

CRISPIN

Look man, you've gotta get out of this mindset. Who cares what people
think it looks like. *We* know there's no sex taking place, don't get so hung
up man.

ALF

Yeah, yeah, it's just, well, some o' The Chaps I knock about with, they're
not as open minded as me. They're not, uh --

CRISPIN

-- *with it?*

ALF

With what?

CRISPIN

(sighing)

Oh it doesn't really matter, Alf. Let's just get on and --

ALF

-- yeah, forget about it. I don't even know why I mentioned it in the first place, but it's better safe than sorry, eh? My Old Mum used to say that all the time she did. Everything that came out her cakehole was "it's better safe than sorry" this, or "it's better safe than sorry" that. Like a bleedin' parrot she was, like one o' those mynah birds, bless her.

(he remembers something)

Here – you'll like this, funny story -- there's this one time we was down Billericay and --

CRISPIN FROWNS, SIGHS AND CHECKS HIS WATCH. HE SNAPS AT ALF.

CRISPIN

-- Alf! Please. Can we just get on?

ALF

Oh, uh --

CRISPIN

-- are you good, Alf? Can we do it now, please?

ALF COMPOSES HIMSELF, PSYCHES HIMSELF UP.

ALF

Yeah, yeah, I'm good as gold I am. Never been better. I'm in rude health I am. Tip top and ship shape.
(quietly)
Fuckin' fifty sovs lighter mind.

CRISPIN

Right, let's do it then.

ALF TAKES A DEEP BREATH, PUTS HIS
HANDS ON HIS Y-FRONTS, CLOSES HIS
EYES AND JUST AS HE IS ABOUT TO
PULL THEM DOWN ...

ALF

Yeah ... in for a penny ... you can have yer pound o' flesh, son, don't *you* worry ... let's get it over with ... I'm just gonna close me eyes ...
(takes a deep breath, limbers
up)
I'm just gonna close me eyes n' pretend this ain't happening ... I'm gonna think of England n' our good old Queen, bless her ... I'm gonna pretend I'm actin' I am.

JUST AS ALF IS ABOUT TO EXPOSE
HIMSELF ...

LIGHTS DOWN

The song 'An Actors Life For Me'
from Pinocchio plays.

The Secret Life of the Novel

"A unique metaphysical noir that reads like a map to the subconscious."
Irvine Welsh

A militant atheist Scientist working at the CERN laboratory in Switzerland tries to make the flesh into Word whilst a Scotland Yard Detective is sent to Ibiza to investigate a ritual mass murder that never took place. Time is shown to be fragmenting before our very eyes as Unreliable Narrators, Homicidal Wannabe Authors, Metaphysical Tricksters & Lost Souls haunt the near life experiences of an Ampersand who is trying to collect memories to finish a novel nobody will ever read. Goat Killers, Apocalyptic Pirate Radio DJ's, Dead Pop Stars, Social Engineers and Cartoon Characters populate a twilight landscape that may or may not exist depending on who's narrating at the time.

The Secret Life Of The Novel is a meditation on time, creation and memory that leaves the reader questioning whether they may have been unconsciously complicit in the rewriting of History.

Book One of ZANI's Tales Trilogy

A CRAFTY CIGARETTE
TALES OF A TEENAGE MOD

Foreword by John Cooper Clarke.
'I couldn't put it down because I couldn't put it down.'

'Crafty Cigarette, all things Mod and a dash of anarchy. Want to remember what it was like to be young and angry? Buy this book. A great read.'
Phil Davis (Actor Chalky in Quadrophenia)

'A Great Debut That Deals With The Joys and Pains of Growing Up.'
Irvine Welsh

'A coming of age story, 'A Crafty Cigarette' maybe Matteo Sedazzari's debut novel but it's an impressive story.'
Vive Le Rock

'It's a good book and an easy read. That's pretty much what most pulp fiction needs to be.'
Mod Culture

'A work of genius.'
Alan McGee (Creation Records)

'Like a good Paul Weller concert the novel leaves you wanting more. I'll be very interested in reading whatever Matteo Sedazzari writes next.'
Louder Than War

A mischievous youth prone to naughtiness, he takes to mod like a moth to a flame, which in turn gives him a voice, confidence and a fresh new outlook towards life, his family, his school friends, girls and the world in general. Growing up in Sunbury–on–Thames where he finds life rather dull and hard to make friends, he moves across the river with his family to Walton–on–Thames in 1979, the year of the Mod Revival, where to his delight he finds many other Mods his age and older, and slowly but surely he starts to become accepted...."

A Crafty Cigarette is the powerful story of a teenager coming of age in the 70s as seen through his eyes, who on the cusp of adulthood, discovers a band that is new to him, which leads him into becoming a Mod.

ISBN-13 : 978-1526203564

Book Two of ZANI's Tales Trilogy

THE MAGNIFICENT SIX
IN TALES OF AGGRO

Foreword by Drummer Steve White (The Style Council, Paul Weller, Trio Valore,)
'A vivid and enjoyable slice of London life in the 80s, with a wealth of detail and characters,'

'Tales of Aggro is a kind of time machine that takes one back to the days of 'Scrubbers', 'Scum' and 'Get Carter'. Very redolent of those atmospherics.'
Jonathan Holloway – Theatre Director and Playwright

The **MagNiFiceNt**

in tales of aggro

Matteo Sedazzari

'Tales of Aggro has got the feel of 'Green Street' and a touch of 'Lock Stock and Two Smoking Barrels'. This is fiction for realists.'
Vive Le Rock

'A real slice of life told in the vernacular of the streets'
Irvine Welsh

'Laugh out loud funny, exciting and above all, written with real warmth and passion for London and the Character's making their way through this tale and life itself.'
Gents of London

'It's A Treat to Read, Just Like A Crafty Cigarette'
John Cooper Clarke

'Tales of Aggro is lively and funny'
Phil Davis (British Actor – Quadrophenia, Silk, The Firm)

'Tales of Aggro is a kind of time machine that takes one back to the days of 'Scrubbers', 'Scum' and 'Get Carter'. Very redolent of those atmospherics.'
Jonathan Holloway – Theatre Director and Playwright

Meet Oscar De Paul, Eddie the Casual, Dino, Quicksilver, Jamie Joe and Honest Ron, collectively known around the streets of West London as The Magnificent Six. This gang of working-class lovable rogues have claimed Shepherds Bush and White City as their playground and are not going to let anyone spoil the fun.

Meet Stephanie, a wannabe pop star who is determined to knock spots off the Spice Girls, with her girl group. Above all though, meet West London and hear the stories of ordinary people getting up to extraordinary adventures.

Please note that Tales of Aggro is a work of fiction.

ISBN-13 : 978-1527235823

Book Three of ZANI's Tales Trilogy

TALES FROM THE
FOXES OF FOXHAM

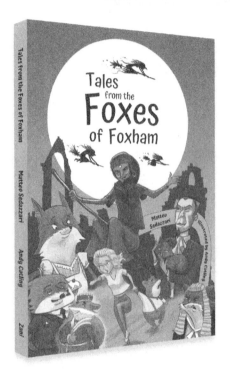

It is the late fifties and the Witches of Benevento are determined to plunge the world into darkness by kidnapping and sacrificing the jolly and young Neapolitan fox, Alberto Bandito, in a sinister ritual.

Yet, fortunately for Alberto, he is rescued, then guarded, by his loving mother Silvia and mob boss father Mario with his troops, a good witch Carlotta with an uncanny resemblance to Marilyn Monroe, the Bears of Campania, the boxing wolves' brothers Francesco and Leonardo, and other good folks of Naples and beyond.

However, their protection is not enough, for Alberto has been cursed. So, the young fox, along with his family, has to travel to the village of Foxham in Norfolk, the spiritual home of foxes across the world, to rid himself of this spell. The ritual has to be performed by a good fox witch, Trudi Milanese, but there is a problem, Trudi doesn't know she is a witch....

Tales from The Foxes of Foxham is a magical adventure story, packed with colourful characters and exciting situations, in a battle of good versus evil.

ISBN-13 : 978-1838462420

MORE BOOKS FROM ZANI
www.zani.co.uk

Feltham Made Me – Paolo Sedazzari
Foreword by Mark Savage (Grange Hill)

The poet Richard F. Burton likened the truth to a large mirror, shattered into millions upon millions of pieces. Each of us owns a piece of that mirror, believing our one piece to be the whole truth. But you only get to see the whole truth when we put all the pieces together. This is the concept behind Feltham Made Me. It is the story of three lads growing up together in the suburbs of London, put together from the transcripts of many hours of interview.

ISBN-13 : 978-1527210608

The Secret Life Of The Novel: Faking Your Death is Illegal, Faking Your Life is Celebrated - Dean Cavanagh

"A unique metaphysical noir that reads like a map to the subconscious." **Irvine Welsh**

A militant atheist Scientist working at the CERN laboratory in Switzerland tries to make the flesh into Word whilst a Scotland Yard Detective is sent to Ibiza to investigate a ritual mass murder that never took place. Time is shown to be fragmenting before our very eyes as Unreliable Narrators, Homicidal Wannabe Authors, Metaphysical Tricksters & Lost Souls haunt the near life experiences of an Ampersand who is trying to collect memories to finish a novel nobody will ever read. Goat Killers, Apocalyptic Pirate Radio DJ's, Dead Pop Stars, Social Engineers and Cartoon Characters populate a twilight landscape that may or may not exist depending on who's narrating at the time.

ISBN-13 : 978-1527201538

7P'S Paperback – A.G.R

The 7 P's. An unusual title you may think, but its meaning will become as apparent to you as it did for four friends and comrades who, in a desperate move of self-preservation, escaped the troubles of 1980s Northern Ireland, and their hometown of Belfast, only to find themselves just as deep, if not deeper, in trouble of a different kind on the treacherous streets of London.

ISBN-13 : 978-1527258365

ZANI ON SOCIAL MEDIA

After enjoying *Tales from The Foxes of Foxham,* please follow ZANI on Social Media.

ZANI is a passionate and quirky entertaining online magazine covering contemporary, counter and popular culture.

Follow ZANI on Twitter
twitter.com/ZANIEzine

Follow ZANI on FaceBook
www.facebook.com/zanionline?fref=ts

Follow ZANI on Instagram
www.instagram.com/zanionline/

Printed in Great Britain
by Amazon

87059365R00088